37388

Willard W. Cochrane is a professor of agricultural economics at the University of Minnesota. He previously served as an economist with the Food and Agriculture Organization of the United Nations and with the U.S. Department of Agriculture. He is the co-author of two other books, *Economics of American Agriculture* and *Economics of Consumption*.

FARM PRICES

Myth and Reality

Willard W. Cochrane

UNIVERSITY OF MINNESOTA PRESS
Minneapolis

Printed in the United States of America at the
North Central Publishing Company, St. Paul

Library of Congress Catalog Card Number: 58-7556

PUBLISHED IN GREAT BRITAIN, INDIA, AND PAKISTAN BY THE
OXFORD UNIVERSITY PRESS, LONDON, BOMBAY, AND KARACHI
AND IN CANADA BY THOMAS ALLEN, LTD., TORONTO

Preface

THIS book deals with the price-income problems of commercial agriculture in the United States. The number of commercial farms in the United States has been declining in recent years, but in absolute terms the number of such farms remains large. In 1954 there were close to three million farms in the United States, selling products valued at $1000 or more per year. And the price-income problems of this major grouping of farms and farmers has not diminished in recent years.

Lauren Soth, in his interesting little book *Farm Trouble*, contends that one of the fundamental problems of American agriculture is to be found in the one third of American farm families who live in poverty even during boom times. Perhaps he is right; perhaps this third, and not commercial farmers, constitute the basic problem of American agriculture (although there is considerable overlapping of the two groups). And, of course, there are other important problems that could be discussed: the social adjustments of the millions of rural people flocking to the cities, world agricultural developments, and so on. I do not contend that the price-income problems of commercial farmers are the most critical in present-day society. But it is my thesis that these price-income problems are nagging and continuing. Further, certain structural changes within modern society are aggravating and accentuating these problems. Thus, it is the purpose of this book to bring the best in modern analysis — information, economic logic, and social theory — to bear on the price-income problems of commercial agriculture.

Although many new estimates and descriptive measures are presented in the pages that follow, no new concepts, or theories, are developed in those pages. In the main, the book builds on previous work — previous work of the author and other workers in the social disciplines. The novelty of the book, if indeed novelty exists, rests on the organization and relationship of the ideas presented. The information, economic logic, and social theory presented are organized and related in a general conception of the structure and behavior of commercial agriculture in an evolving, developing economy — the general conception of the author.

Now it does not follow, because the ideas of this little volume are linked together by a general conception, or a point of view, that the various facts, estimates of relationships, and concepts are biased. An internally consistent conception of the structure and behavior of commercial agriculture in the total economy, helpful in problem solving, must accommodate itself to the facts, relationships, and human values of the changing world. A man is not only dishonest but a fool to consciously distort data and relationships to fit his preconceptions (although there is probably some of this in the subconscious of each of us); the idea world of such a man must at some point either collapse or take flight into the land of make-believe.

To assume, however, that facts and relationships have meaning outside some point of view or general integrating conception is to err in another direction — in the direction of little wisdom. A set of facts and relations unrelated by a point of view or integrating conception becomes a grab-bag of little known, miscellaneous facts and relationships on some subject. Facts and relationships always exist in some context; thus, for them to be used to describe or explain or represent some situation, they must be related in an integrating conception of that context (in this case commercial agriculture).

In the writing of this book a great deal of time and effort went into trying to reduce difficult and technical relations and concepts to straightforward, understandable language — language that interested and informed laymen (e.g., community leaders and agricultural leaders) could follow. But I was not uniformly successful in this objective; hence noneconomists will probably want to skip over Chapter 4. The main sweep of the argument is not lost in doing so; but those readers interested in trying to unravel the price-output behavior of individual commodities *within* agriculture may find help in Chapter 4.

Along this same line, Chapter 3 may look formidable in spots, but it can be read without too great difficulty. Further, the concepts and estimates presented there will prove interesting to many.

Acknowledgments in a book like this one are difficult. The ideas and the integrating point of view presented have grown with me over at least a decade, and have benefited from the work and writing of many people. Perhaps the men who contributed most to the key ideas and integrating point of view of this book were the author's colleagues in the old, old Bureau of Agricultural Economics: H. R. Tolley, Bushrod W. Allin, James G. Maddox, John M. Brewster, Howard L. Parsons, John A. Baker, and James P. Cavin. The development and sharpening of the conceptual parts have resulted in large measure from the criticisms of, and discussions with, such men as George E. Brandow, Robert L. Clodius, W. W. Wilcox, T. W. Schultz, Roger W. Gray, and J. K. Galbraith.

In the final writing job, numerous people have made contributions. Elmer W. Learn helped think through some of the estimating procedures central to the argument, and he read most of the manuscript for errors large and small; Milo Peterson and Paul H. Hoepner helped with the many calculations and the estimating work; Lee M. Day and John M. Wetmore read most of the manuscript in one of its several versions and made numerous suggestions for improving it; and Barbara Nelson converted my chicken tracks (hardly to be dignified by the term writing) to a clean typewritten manuscript. The beautifully drawn charts, which add to the attractiveness of the book, were done by Doris Olsen. And my wife, as always, contributed to the readability of the text.

Last but not least, a single-quarter leave granted by the University of Minnesota should be acknowledged. This leave enabled me to find the time to put on paper the ideas which comprise this little book.

WILLARD W. COCHRANE

June 1957

Contents

PART I

Farm Price-Income Behavior

1

The Myth

Farm prices are always on the move. Sometimes they fluctuate wildly and in wide swings; sometimes they fluctuate through a fairly regular cycle. But they stay on the move. This kind of price behavior in American agriculture dates back to the Civil War and before. It is not new, and there is little evidence to suggest that it will change in the near future (although in recent years, downswings in certain commodity prices have been moderated by governmental action).

Out of this price variability — regular and irregular, wide and narrow — emerge several farm problems: variable farm incomes, low incomes over extended periods, and uncertainty in planning production. And, although the magnitude of these problems is only vaguely known, the causes poorly understood, and the solutions much debated, the public has been, and continues to be, generally aware of the problems. The awareness is there; the press and politicians have seen to that.

But a widely held myth blankets the public awareness of these problems, and beclouds the issues involved. It is the myth of an automatically adjusting agriculture — an agriculture that tends toward a golden mean. Variant number one, and typically the older variant, of the myth says: There is some desirable level and pattern of prices, production, and incomes for agriculture toward which agriculture would gravitate and stabilize, if it were left alone for a little while. Variant number two, and typically the newer variant, of the myth says: There is some desirable level and pattern of prices, production, and incomes for agriculture toward which agriculture would gravitate and stabilize if it were given a friendly and helping hand, presumably by government.

In other words, in each peacetime agricultural slump, the view is ex-

3

pressed over and over again to this effect: "Agriculture is basically 'sound'; it is just a little out of balance. And if we wait a little while for the necessary adjustments to take place, or pass some 'emergency' legislation to help the necessary adjustments take place, all will be well." This is the myth of a self-adjusting, or easily adjusted, agriculture.

Now the segment of the public sharing the first variant of the myth obviously differs from that holding to the second variant. The first variant is largely held by small businessmen who do not benefit from any kind of governmental assistance and somehow manage to get along, by the big business community which often benefits from government contracts and subsidies but which does not like too much government in business — particularly not the regulatory type, and by those people who yearn for the good old days — preferably pre-McKinley. The second variant is more often held by farmers themselves and their spokesmen, labor and labor leaders, politicians of the New Deal and Fair Deal persuasion, and persons tainted by these latter-day persuasions.

The divergence in belief of the two groups should not, however, be overemphasized; the divergence that exists is with respect to mechanics, not basic belief. Both groups share the core of the myth. They hold in common that (1) there is some stable, optimum level and pattern of prices, incomes, and production for agriculture; (2) this optimum level and pattern is knowable (i.e., may be specified in quantitative terms from history, or statistics, or some other discipline); and (3) with some "straight" thinking and action agriculture could and would move to this optimum level and pattern of prices, production, and incomes *and then stay there.* This is central to the myth — some "sound" thinking and action would put agriculture back on the "right track" and thereafter agriculture would of its own accord run in the grooves of this "right track."

Some variant of the automatic myth runs through the writings and speeches of most present-day politicians, farm leaders, and informed laymen. But people who live by a myth obviously do not describe it as such. If they did, the myth would cease to exist. Rather they talk about and write about their beliefs, their faith, and their logical conclusions. Further, they talk and write in some context for some purpose. Thus, in the illustrative materials presented below, the committee members are concerned with developing a set of policy recommendations for dealing with the farm problem, not with recording a myth. The myth is implicit,

4

however, in every line quoted, and in the longer report from which the quotations are taken.

The report in question was prepared for The Twentieth Century Fund by a committee of twelve nationally known persons [1] in the field of agriculture and is appended to the volume *Can We Solve the Farm Problem?* by Murray R. Benedict. Since this committee was composed of reasonable and modern men and women, they prepared a reasonably modern report. The myth that threads through it is not the first, or older, variant; it is the recent, or newer, variant. They make clear that

If steps designed to maintain prosperity and high employment generally are not taken, or if they prove unsuccessful, emergency programs in both the farm and nonfarm sectors are appropriate . . .

and they go on to say

When programs designed to meet abnormal national needs cause severe distortions in the agricultural economy, as in wartime, the national government has an obligation to assist in the transition to a more balanced pattern of output in the succeeding period and should accept that responsibility.

Thus, they are willing to give agriculture a friendly and helping hand during emergencies, but

Such types of aid . . . should not be of such a nature or so long continued as to perpetuate the unbalance in the agricultural economy. They should be accompanied by positive programs designed to provide opportunity and incentives for changes in production that will bring output into line with demand in the national and international markets, plus such amounts of farm products as may be required for other programs that may be agreed on.

And they continue in a more positive vein:

In the suggestions made, we recognize that government has an important role to play in stabilizing and strengthening the agricultural economy, but we favor as much reliance on automatic adjustments in the market as is consistent with the goals suggested. We believe that the farmers of the United States want, and that the general welfare requires, an agricultural economy in which there will be as much freedom of action as is consistent with the maintenance of reasonable stability and

[1] They were Jesse W. Tapp, Chairman, John D. Black, Harry B. Caldwell, Calvin B. Hoover, Donald R. Murphy, Edwin G. Nourse, Margaret G. Reid, Quentin Reynolds, Theodore W. Schultz, Andrew Stewart, Louise Leonard Wright, and Obed A. Wyum. It should be noted, however, that Harry B. Caldwell and Donald R. Murphy dissented from the report in a vigorous statement.

5

equality of opportunity between farming and other occupations. The contribution which can be made by the wisdom and managerial ability of some five million farm operators should not be sacrificed through too much reliance on regulation and centralized planning, which inevitably draw on relatively small numbers of brains and create inefficiencies and inconsistencies in an economy as diverse and complex as ours.

Most of the adjustments needed are not uniform but instead should vary from farm to farm, depending on the particular situation. They can best be brought about through full use of the vast reservoir of managerial ability that exists in the farmers of the United States. Such action, participated in by millions of farmers, brought about many of the great shifts and readjustments of the past: the shift out of wheat, beef cattle and sheep in the New England area; the development of the great dairy and livestock industries of the Middle West; and the grain and specialty-crop industries of the Plains area and the Far West. Farmers, through their individual action, brought into use mechanized agriculture, hybrid corn, improved breeds of livestock, and many other new developments.

And they breathe new life into the myth in the following statement referring to occupational mobility:

Such adjustments, even today, occur too slowly and too incompletely to maintain full equality of returns and opportunities in the farm and nonfarm parts of the economy. However, if freedom of choice to work either in agriculture or out of it can be achieved and maintained, *real incomes to farmers should not long remain far out of balance with real incomes in comparable nonfarm occupations* even though urban workers and industries may have somewhat more direct control over prices and incomes than have farmers.[2]

Many other examples of the myth could be presented, and more pungent ones — particularly from the speeches of politicians. But in the Committee Report of The Twentieth Century Fund we view the myth in its most modern and appealing dress. All of the basic ingredients of the myth remain, however: the emergency character of the farm problem; the desirable level and pattern of prices, production, and incomes to get back to; and the "right" action on the part of several million farmers that will best direct the agricultural industry back to that desirable situation.

It should be clear by this time that the myth we are talking about is not the agrarian myth of the eighteenth and nineteenth centuries; it

[2] These quotations are from the Committee Report of *Can We Solve the Farm Problem?* (New York: The Twentieth Century Fund, 1955), pp. 488–494; italics mine.

6

is not remotely related to the Jeffersonian idyl. The agrarian myth was, and to the extent that it still exists, is concerned with the supposed virtues of rural, or farm, life; Richard Hofstadter sums up the essence of that myth in a few lines:

. . . Its hero was the yeoman farmer, its central conception the notion that he is the ideal man and the ideal citizen. . . . The yeoman, who owned a small farm and worked it with the aid of his family, was the incarnation of the simple, honest, independent, healthy, happy human being. Because he lived in close communion with beneficent nature, his life was believed to have a wholesomeness and integrity impossible for the depraved populations of cities. His well-being was not merely physical, it was moral; it was not merely personal, it was the central source of civic virtue; it was not merely secular but religious, for God had made the land and called man to cultivate it. . . .[3]

The myth of a self-adjusting, or easily adjusted, agriculture, grows out of a different tradition; it grows out of the nonfarm, commercial interests in American society; the complex of ideas comprising this myth was formulated in urban centers by spokesmen for commercial interests — by David Ricardo, William Graham Sumner, and Herbert Hoover. In short, it is the doctrine of *laissez faire* applied to agriculture. And, although this doctrine has been eroded away under corporate bigness and governmental intervention in the economy generally, the doctrine still has vitality for agriculture. The second, and now dominant variant of the automatic myth testifies to this vitality.

The historic perversity of agriculture in straying from the path of stable, orderly development must, however, be explained in some way. The people, the farmers, who suffer and prosper as a part of these wayward processes demand some sort of an explanation. The usual explanation supplied runs in terms of a blame theory; someone, or something, it is argued, is at fault for the plight of the farmer. Older blame theories, such as big business monopolies, Wall Street, and the trickery of middlemen, are indigenous to agriculture itself; in the main they grow out of farm discontent and the agrarian revolts of the latter half of the nineteenth century. But more recent blame theories, foreign trade difficulties, "unsound" political action, and war and its aftermath, have been supplied by commercial "experts" with interests in agriculture — the banker on Main Street, the successful corporation executive, and more recently agricultural economists.

[3] *The Age of Reform: From Bryan to F.D.R.* (New York: Alfred A. Knopf, 1956), p. 24.

Farm Price-Income Behavior

Depending on the time and place, each of these blame theories has gained widespread acceptance. Granted the myth, this must be the case. Someone or something must be to blame, otherwise agriculture would currently be moving along the path of stable, orderly development as the result of some past "sound" thinking and action.

The development of the complex of ideas entering into the myth of a self-adjusting, or easily adjusted, agriculture has obviously been a lengthy and complex affair. And the unraveling of this idea complex is beyond the purview of this little book. But the general idea seems to be fed by three ideological streams in the American experience. First, most Americans maintain an attitude of economic optimism — an attitude consistent with, and growing out of, a century and a half of unparalleled economic growth involving territorial expansion, technological advance, and rising real incomes. Thus it is natural for the layman to be optimistic about the farm problem — to believe that this is just one more tough economic problem that can be solved and, once solved, that it will stay solved (it is interesting to observe in this connection that an attitude born of expansion runs into difficulty as it encounters a contracting industry).

Second, some of the most disastrous price-income swings in American agriculture have followed wars. Thus, it is commonplace to ascribe these price-income declines to the wars that preceded them. In this line of reasoning, war is the culprit; the dramatic dislocations of war cause agriculture to get out of balance, and assistance is required to get it back in balance. But important to the automatic myth — its origin and acceptance — is the idea that agriculture did not get out of balance of its own accord, or because of normal or natural causes; the abnormalities of war drove it out of balance. Hence the inference is that if there had not been war, agriculture would be moving along the path of stable, orderly development.

Third, one hundred and fifty years of orthodox economic theory provides the myth with an economic rationale. Everyone who has suffered through a first course in principles of economics will recall the famous Marshallian cross and its automatic process: a demand curve sloping downward and to the right, and a supply curve sloping upward and to the right effecting a point of intersection with demand. Price, it will be recalled, is always tending toward the point of intersection, as excess demand below the intersection drives price up, and excess supply above

8

the intersection pushes price down.[4] Thus, the workings of the impersonal and automatic forces of demand and supply, commodity by commodity and factor by factor, guide the economy, integrate its many pieces and processes, and stabilize it (i.e., dampen down explosive behavior). And since agriculture is one part of this economy, it is presumed that the "unseen hand" operates to guide and stabilize agriculture too — in the aggregate and by commodities.

For the economy to behave in practice as the above theory says it should, several important conditions must, however, be satisfied: (1) the economy must be comprised of many small units — many buyers and many sellers; (2) each commodity and factor must have some, or many, close substitutes; and (3) products and factors must be mobile — barriers to mobility must be at a minimum. The fact that these conditions often are not satisfied in the real world, and that the operating economy has throughout modern times received many assists from government, has not destroyed the myth as far as agriculture is concerned. Economic reality may have damaged the myth somewhat and produced the second variant. But the core of the myth remains intact, and it is sustained and given an inner logic by traditional economic theory.

Other elements have perhaps entered into the creation and dissemination of the myth of an automatically adjusting agriculture. But the three ideological streams described above have contributed importantly to it. Acting and interacting, these idea patterns have provided the foundation stones of the myth: the optimistic attitude, the exception created of war, the logical bases. In this combination the myth could grow and survive, and it has.

[4] The conventional demand and supply cross is portrayed in the accompanying diagram. The forces of supply and demand cause price to move toward and become established at point P. Any price above point P will not hold because excess supply drives it down; any price below point P will not hold because excess demand drives it up. Only the price and quantity established by the intersection of supply and demand at point P are stable and have no tendency to change; hence they are defined as the equilibrium price and quantity.

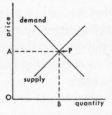

9

2

The Reality

BELIEF plays an important role in the lives of men — guiding the faithful; and theory is an indispensable part of the scientific method — guiding particular inquiries. But there comes a time when belief and theory must encounter reality. Sometimes reality is thrust upon the faithful and theoreticians from the outside, and sometimes the faithful and theoreticians go seeking the real world. But always the comparison must come — a comparison between what is believed, or hypothesized, and reality — wherein the beliefs and theories hold up and are substantiated, or they fail to meet the test of reality and are proven wrong.

Now it is when beliefs and theories turn out to be inconsistent with, or in conflict with, the facts of the real world that trouble arises. In some cases people are so wedded to their beliefs, or theories, that they will not, or cannot, discard them when proven wrong. For these individuals beliefs and theories are more real than the phenomena. It is at this point that fancy takes over and a mythology comes into being. And this is what we find in agriculture: a belief concerning its inherent stability, or orderliness, that refuses to crumble before the reality of price-income instability. To this deeply held belief may be given the name the Myth of an Automatically Adjusting Agriculture (the three A's in a different context).

Actually, the roller-coaster-like behavior of farm prices and incomes has been observed time and time again. And, of course, farm people have felt these dramatic price-income sweeps time and time again — sometimes enjoying the ride, sometimes crying out for help. The data describing farm price-income behavior have been collected, refined, and observed; and the experiences of farm people have been told and retold, but still the myth persists. The task of this chapter is to confront the myth once again, and this time head on, with the facts of price-income instability in agriculture.

The Long View of Farm Prices, 1826–1956

The level of farm product prices gyrates through time in a spectacular and uncertain fashion, and it has for well over a hundred years (see Figure 1).[1] The level of farm prices in the United States, and of nonfarm prices as well, is dominated over the long run by the upheavals of three great wars: the Civil War, World War I, and World War II. The crests in product prices generally are realized during and immediately following great wars. But between these war periods the farm price level bobs along in a fashion peculiar to itself.

It is interesting to observe that farm prices and nonfarm prices behave in a similar fashion in only one kind of historical period, a kind of period that we generally consider to be abnormal, namely, wartime. The farm price level and the nonfarm price level rise and fall in a parallel fashion in both the Civil War and World War I. The magnitudes involved, as well as the configuration of the movements, are strikingly similar for both price levels in each of these periods. And taking into account the heroic, but uneven, efforts to control prices during World War II, the behavior of farm and nonfarm prices is not too dissimilar in the latter war period.

It is in peacetime that the unique and unstable aspects of the farm price level manifest themselves. Before the Civil War, the level of farm prices fluctuates in an unruly fashion, with farm prices falling, or rising, by as much as 20 to 30 per cent over a period of a year or two. In the long post–Civil War price decline, farm prices exhibit a "bumptious" quality, fluctuating in the short run to a greater extent than do nonfarm prices. In the fifteen-year period leading up to the Golden Age of American agriculture, 1910–14, farm prices rose at a considerably more rapid rate than did nonfarm prices. The stability of both farm and nonfarm prices, and the equality of the two indices in Figure 1 for the period

[1] The data in Figure 1 are plotted on a ratio, or semi-logarithmic, chart. This type of chart facilitates comparisons between rates of change, or changes occurring from different base levels. For example, an increase from 50 to 100 on this type of chart shows up as large as an increase from 100 to 200, because proportionately it is as large. In all other cases in this volume where direct comparisons are important, semi-logarithmic charts are used.

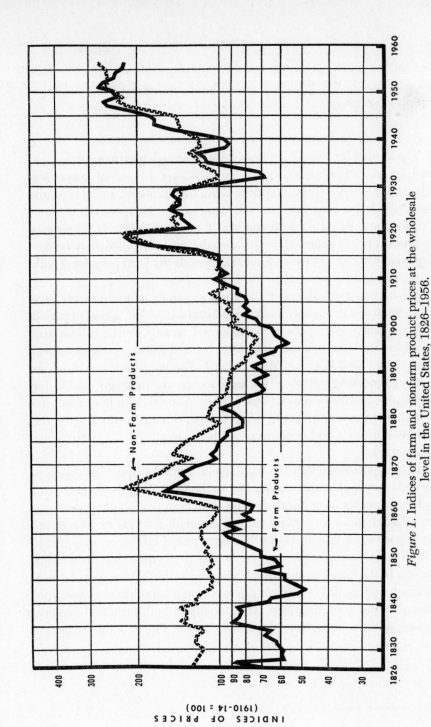

Figure 1. Indices of farm and nonfarm product prices at the wholesale level in the United States, 1826–1956.

INDICES OF PRICES
(1910-14 = 100)

12

1910–14, are induced in large measure by the mechanics of index number construction. (Since the *average prices* for that five-year period are defined as 100 for each index, each year's index value during that period tends to approximate 100.) Between World Wars I and II agriculture experienced some of the most precipitous price declines and dramatic price upturns ever experienced in history. And now following the hot "police action" in Korea, farm prices are once again on the skids, even though these same farm prices are protected by various governmental price supporting operations.

Offhand it does not appear that war plays any favorites. Both farm and nonfarm prices rise and fall together in wartime. It is in peacetime that differences emerge. In periods of economic recovery, farm prices generally rise first, and they generally rise the most; in periods of economic downturn farm prices generally fall first, and they *always* fall the farthest. Farm prices, it seems, are at the crack end of the whip, rising and falling dramatically with any small change in over-all business activity. And it should be noted with more than academic interest that the amplitude and the frequency of farm price level fluctuations have increased since World War I. This is not accidental as we shall discover in Part II; there are solid economic reasons for this increasing variability.

The Frayed Rope, 1910–56

Since most of us are more interested in the recent past than in the distant past, let us look more closely at the behavior of farm prices since 1910. The complex of lines running across Figure 2, which looks something like a frayed rope, describes the behavior of farm prices since 1910 reasonably well. The heavy line at the center of the frayed rope describes movements in the farm price level; it does this because it is the graphic representation of the average of all farm prices (it is in fact the regularly published series, the Index of Prices Received by Farmers for All Commodities).[2] The differently symbolled lines, or frayed ends, show variations in commodity prices around the moving farm price level (for nine of the more important farm commodities). These individual commodity price lines indicate the extent to which individual commodity prices parallel movements of the level, and the extent to which they vary around it.

[2] The source is relevant issues of *Agricultural Statistics*, U.S. Department of Agriculture.

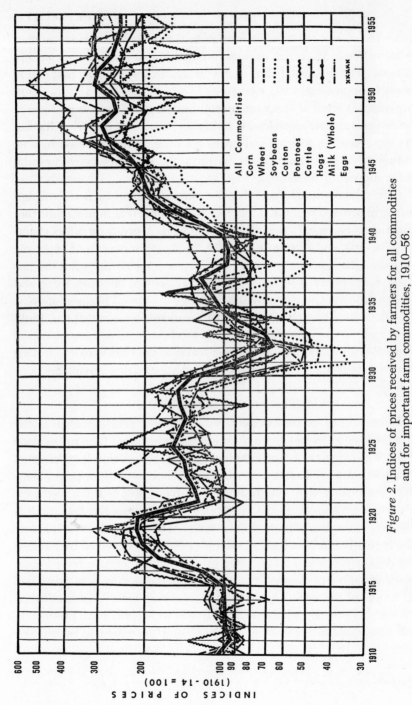

Figure 2. Indices of prices received by farmers for all commodities and for important farm commodities, 1910–56.

INDICES OF PRICES (1910–14 = 100)

14

Even a casual inspection of Figure 2 suggests that there are two different kinds of price variability in agriculture: (1) wide swings in the farm price level, and (2) year-to-year variations in commodity prices around the moving farm price level.

The farm price level is an unstable thing moving through time in broad and dramatic sweeps. No rhythmic pattern, or periodicity, is discernible in these sweeps. The upswings are associated with economic recovery and hot wars; the downswings are associated with economic depressions and postwar periods. To illustrate: the level of prices received by farmers fell 43 per cent between 1919 and 1921, fell another 56 per cent between 1929 and 1932, rose 185 per cent between 1940 and 1948, and fell again by 22 per cent between 1951 and 1955. And this last decline was moderated by various governmental price supporting actions. We can therefore conclude that the farm price level fluctuates in the extreme, and that these fluctuations follow no predictable pattern.

A different story emerges with respect to the year-to-year variations in farm commodity prices around the moving farm price level. Some commodity prices move in close harmony with the over-all level, others fluctuate wildly about it. This can be seen in Figure 2. Whole milk prices, for example, move right along with the farm price level; potato prices, on the other hand, fluctuate wildly about it. And most other farm commodities fall somewhere between these two.

Estimates of year-to-year price variability for fifteen important farm commodities are shown in Table 1. These estimates, average percentages for periods between 1920 and 1955, describe the extent of year-to-year price variations in particular commodities, where the influence of changes in the farm price level have been removed. In other words, these estimates describe in percentage terms the amount of year-to-year price variability remaining to individual farm commodities where the heavy black price level line in Figure 2 is visualized as a perfectly horizontal line.

For the period 1920–55, the average year-to-year percentage variation in the price of whole milk around the farm price level is 6 per cent (Table 1), of hogs 15 per cent, of cotton 19 per cent, and of potatoes 48 per cent. In other words, in each year between 1920 and 1955 the price of whole milk changed, on the average, 6 per cent, either increasing or decreasing, as measured from the farm price level. Similarly with respect to hogs and every other commodity listed in Table 1. The estimates in Table 1 indicate the average percentage price change, in either direction, that occurred for each commodity each year around the moving farm price level (over and above any changes in the farm price level). It is interesting to observe from Table 1 that the degree of year-to-year commodity price variability is reduced substantially during the period 1943–55, when price supporting actions were common in agriculture. Whatever else governmental price supports did, and we shall consider this in Part III, price supporting actions obviously reduced the year-to-year price variability of such commodities as wheat, cotton, corn, tobacco, and potatoes.

Table 1. Year-to-Year Percentage Variations in the Prices of Important Farm Commodities around the Moving Farm Price Level, Averages for Selected Periods *

Commodity	1920–33	1934–42	1943–55	1920–55
Whole milk	7.39	5.13	5.41	6.11
Butterfat in cream	6.02	5.56	5.73	5.80
Eggs	7.20	9.01	13.25	9.84
Soybeans	21.96†	26.21	11.41	19.21
Hogs	14.59	20.54	12.54	15.34
Wheat	19.76	16.16	5.54	13.73
Cotton	32.39	15.95	7.44	19.27
Corn	20.45	22.68	11.56	17.80
Oats	17.98	31.82	11.68	19.17
Tobacco	28.69	22.40	8.99	20.00
Beef cattle	8.53	11.13	9.98	9.70
Apples	36.07	33.18	27.82	32.37
Potatoes	57.86	51.13	37.21	48.72
Oranges	52.64	22.11	27.48	35.92
Onions	63.11	32.94	69.56	57.90

* Individual commodity prices are deflated by the Index of Prices Received by Farmers for All Commodities. Estimates for each period were derived by computing link relatives, then computing the reciprocals of the link relatives below 100, and taking the unweighted arithmetic mean of the resultant numbers, all of which are 100 or more. An index of 100 represents no variation under this computation; hence 100 is subtracted from these results to obtain the percentage values shown above.

† This series originated in 1924; the period covered is therefore 1924–33.

In general, what we observe in Table 1 is a continuum of commodity price variability around the farm price level: from rather modest for whole milk, to substantial for cotton, corn, and wheat, to very great for potatoes, onions, and oranges. Now assume for the moment that no price level problem existed (i.e., that the heavy price level line in Figure

2 is perfectly horizontal); in this unlikely event the 6 per cent change in the price of whole milk from year to year, in either direction, would not be too difficult to live with. But the 15 to 20 per cent changes in the prices of wheat, hogs, corn, and cotton from year to year, in either direction, create a highly uncertain and disturbing environment in which to plan and work. And the 50 to 60 per cent changes in the prices of potatoes and onions from year to year, in either direction, speak for themselves.

Now superimpose this pattern of year-to-year commodity price variability upon a farm price level, which does, in fact, move in wide and dramatic swings, and an economic situation for agriculture emerges that is both highly uncertain and intolerable. This price experience might be likened to a ride on a roller coaster where the individual cars (commodity prices) bob up and down in an uneven and uncertain fashion as the entire train sweeps up and down the roller-coaster track. The experience is just too exhilarating.

Two Economic Problems

The different forms of price variability isolated in the preceding section lead to two different kinds of economic problems. Farm price level fluctuations lead to a general *income problem* in agriculture. The year-to-year variations in farm commodity prices around the moving price level lead to an *uncertainty problem* with implications for resource use and farm business planning. Typically, farmers, politicians, and interested laymen do not distinguish between these two problems, and economists seem to be hypnotized by the second problem. As a result, the first problem rarely is presented in a clear and reasoned form, and the fact that there are two problems is glossed over by laymen and economists alike. We shall try, therefore, to isolate and define the nature of these two price-induced farm problems in this section.[3]

When the farm price level swings upward, or downward, in a major movement, farm commodity prices pull together and move as a unit. Witness the periods 1919–21, 1929–32, and 1940–48 in Figure 2. In these

[3] Actually these two problems are not completely independent. The great swings in the farm price level lead to uncertainty in long-range resource planning, and commodity price variations around the moving farm price level have certain income effects. As in so many cases, these problems are separated by a matter of degree, not by a clear line. But the degree of difference is important in this case.

periods the idea of a level is meaningful; most commodity prices follow the same path. The price level movement of the period 1940–48 obviously does not lead to a farm problem, but it does lead to a general income consequence. This was a period of a pure joyride for farmers; any commodity that a farmer turned to, any alternative that he chose, made him money. This had to be the case, for *all* farm commodity prices were rising together. Thus, all farmers, the efficient and the inefficient, benefited from a farm price level that rose 185 per cent in eight years.

This was not a pure joyride for consumers, however. The great upward sweep in farm prices pinched consumers, and pinched some of them rather hard. This is the opposite side of a general and highly advantageous income consequence for agriculture; this is the short food supply and soaring food price problem, and on occasions it can be a tough, even terrifying, problem. Witness the annoyances experienced by consumers in the United States during the brief period of price ceilings, rationing, and food "shortages" from 1943 to 1945, and the really grave problems encountered by European countries along these lines during and following World War II.

The price level movements of the periods 1919–21 and 1929–32 lead also to general income consequences, but with disastrous consequences for farmers in these cases. When farm commodity prices fall *generally* as they did in the price level declines of 1919–21 and 1929–32, farmers can find no place to hide, no place to take cover. Whichever way the farmer turns, whichever alternative he selects, leads to like results — lower prices and lower income. This is the general income problem of agriculture that terrifies farm people.

The period 1951–56 is not so clear-cut as some of the earlier periods are (see Figure 2). The Index of Prices Received by Farmers for All Commodities, as a measure of the farm price level, falls during this period, and substantially so. But individual commodity prices do not pull together and fall as precipitously as they do in earlier declines. This is due in large measure to the actions taken by government to support the prices of wheat, cotton, corn, and other commodities, and to the use made of supply controls in the tobacco, milk, and sugar markets. Without these various price-supporting and supply-controlling actions, the level of farm prices would have been much lower in 1956 than it was — perhaps 30 to 40 per cent lower (see discussion in Chapter 3), and a parallel downward movement in individual commodity prices would have been in evidence. The general income problem remains; it has simply been blunted by collective action for the first time.

If there were no general income problem in agriculture (i.e., if the price level line in Figure 2 were perfectly horizontal) there would still remain the price uncertainty problem. This problem grows out of the year-to-year commodity price/gyrations around the farm price level, as observed in the previous section. A commodity price may rise one year and fall the next, may rise for two years and fall for one, may rise for one and fall for two; the combinations are not infinite in number, but they are many and they are random. To the farmer next year's price is *uncertain*. He does not know with any reasonable degree of probability whether the price of a particular commodity will be up or down next year, or by how much. Thus he plans for next year's production pretty much in the dark — on a guess here and a hunch there. In this sense these commodity price gyrations around the price level constitute a problem.

This condition of price uncertainty, which, we have observed, is acute in some commodities, leads to a poor, or inefficient, distribution of resources through time in some commodities and to a poor, or inefficient, use of resources among commodities in given time periods. An inefficient use of resources through time results when farmers assume that a high price for a particular commodity in the current year will continue into the second year, and farmers generally transfer resources from alternative enterprises into the increased production of the commodity in question. But the increased production of this commodity in the second year causes its price to fall in that year. Thus, prices and production in this commodity oscillate through time — high price to low price, short production to excessive production.

An inefficient use of resources occurs among commodities, and on individual farms, when farmers fail to use their productive resources in their most advantageous enterprises, because before the fact they do not know which are the most advantageous enterprises. In other words, the best use of resources is not determinable until product prices a year hence are determined. Confronted by this kind of uncertainty, farmers sometimes seek through diversification (where this diversification would be uneconomic if prices were certain) to spread the price risk in agriculture over several commodities and in this manner minimize the income risk from any one. Thus, price uncertainty arising out of

19

commodity price variability in turn gives rise to a widespread malallo-cation of resources in agriculture. And, although this kind of problem generally does not make or break the farmer, it is a constant source of irritation and frustration to him, and it leads to something less than the commonly accepted goal of maximum satisfaction to society from the use of a given set of resources.

Now when the year-to-year variations in commodity prices are super-imposed on the roller-coaster-like movements of the farm price level, as in fact they are in the real world, farmers and other laymen do not see two problems: (1) a general income problem and (2) the ubiquitous resource-allocation problem. What they feel and see is a jumbled, intol-erable price mess — a mess they want resolved to their advantage. But there are really two problems here, very different problems with very different implications. And if farmers, and friends of farmers, want to devise effective means for dealing with the adverse consequences of the price fluctuations they feel and see, they should recognize that two different problems, with different consequences, are involved.

The Income Problem

The general income consequences of fluctuations in the farm price level stand out in bold relief in Figure 3. The realized [4] gross farm in-come line of Figure 3 parallels almost identically the farm price level line of Figure 2. Changes in the gross farm income of all farm operators in the United States would thus appear to be explained almost exclu-sively by changes in the level of farm prices. And this is very nearly the case. Assuming farm prices to be causal, and correlating gross farm income with the index of prices received by farmers for all commodities, changes in the index of prices received account for 92 per cent of the changes in gross farm income. As we shall observe in Part II, changes in production play an important role in determining the level of farm prices, and via this route aggregate output affects gross farm income. But in a given year changes in the level of farm prices account for prac-tically all of the changes in gross farm income. [5]

Realized net farm income of all farm operators in the United States

---

[4] The term *realized* means that the income of farm operators (including non-money income and government payments) has not been adjusted for changes in farm inventories.

[5] This will be the case where the aggregate supply function is perfectly in-elastic.

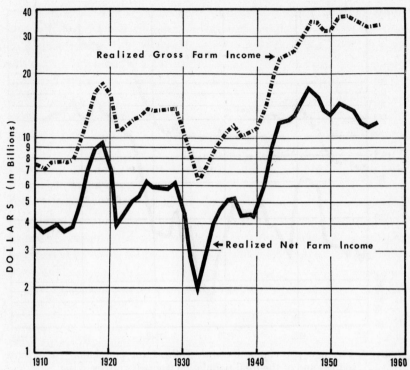

Figure 3. Realized gross and net income from farming of all farm operators in the United States, 1910–56.

behaves in the same general way as does gross farm income (Figure 3). There is, however, one important difference. Changes in net farm income are always a little more extreme than changes in gross farm income. Net farm income slides faster and farther in an economic downturn, and rises faster and farther in an upturn. This follows from the fact that the prices of many production items obtained from the nonfarm sector of the economy are sticky; hence farm production expenses are more rigid than farm product prices. Incidentally, and to keep the record straight, the nonmoney income furnished by farms each year — animal products, the produce of gardens, and the rental value of farm dwellings — is included in the gross and net income series discussed above and portrayed in Figure 3. Also, the nonmoney income furnished by farms is included in the farm per capita series discussed below.

Average per capita incomes of the farm population from farm sources,

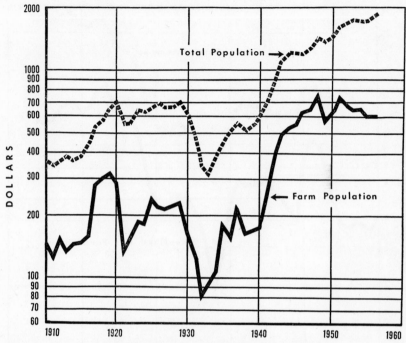

Figure 4. Average per capita income of the farm population from farm
sources and of the total population from all sources in the
United States, 1910–56.

for the period 1910–56, rise and fall in a pattern similar to that of the
total net income of farm operators from farm sources (compare Figures
3 and 4). In other words, putting these farm income data into per capita
terms does not change the farm income picture noticeably. But some
striking differences emerge from a comparison of per capita farm income with per capita incomes for the total population (Figure 4). First,
average per capita incomes of the farm population from farm sources
fluctuate more widely than do average per capita incomes of the total
population — changes in per capita farm incomes are more frequent and
more extreme. Second, per capita farm incomes have declined irregu-
larly since 1948, whereas per capita incomes of the total population have
increased rather steadily since 1948. And third, but not least, per capita
farm incomes on an unadjusted basis have averaged about one third the
size of the per capita incomes of the total population. All in all, the farm
income picture is not a pretty one: wide swings in the farm price level

cause gross farm income to fluctuate widely; sticky production costs cause net farm income to vary even more widely; and average per capita incomes in agriculture are low relative to the total population.

It is sometimes argued that the above comparison between the per capita incomes of the farm population and the total population yields a distorted picture (i.e., makes farm incomes look worse than they really are). People holding this view argue that the existence of large numbers of subsistence farmers — the squirrel-shooters — pulls down estimates of per capita farm income unduly, and that off-farm incomes should be added to the per capita income of the farm population from farm sources. And, depending on the purposes of the comparison, there is validity to both of these arguments. But one wonders at times why people of this persuasion tend always to forget about the low productivity workers in the nonfarm sector.

It should, thus, prove instructive to compare the incomes of *productive* workers whose *principal source of income* is from farming with *productive* workers whose *principal source of income* is from the nonfarm sector. One part of such a comparison may be made without too great difficulty — the comparison of the incomes of families whose principal source of income is from farming with the incomes of families whose principal source of income is from nonfarm pursuits. But limitations of data make the comparison between reasonably productive workers in the two sectors impossible at this time. Families living on low-productive farms — the subsistence farmers, the squirrel-shooters — can be removed from the income averages for agriculture, but little can be done in the way of taking into account the low-productivity people in the nonfarm sector — the aged on retirement plans, the unemployed, and the skid-row characters. For this reason, the comparison that follows is between the average income of commercial farm operator families of all levels of productivity, and the average income of nonfarm families of all levels of productivity.

The average income of nonfarm families in this comparison is simply the average income of all nonfarm families as published from time to time by the U.S. Department of Commerce.[6] The average income of commercial farm operator families is estimated from a 1949 income base, the Census base, for all commercial farm operators, large, medium,

<hr/>

[6] *Income Distribution in the United States, by Size, 1944–50.* A Supplement to the *Survey of Current Business,* 1953, pp. 82–84; *Survey of Current Business,* March 1955, pp. 25–28; and *Survey of Current Business,* June 1956, pp. 13–15.

and small, *but excluding all part-time and residential farms.*[7] The exclusion of these farms yields an average income for those farmers whose principal business is farming. But the average includes estimates of off-farm incomes; hence the concept, average income of commercial farm operator families, includes income from all sources. The *mean* average estimates of farm and nonfarm family incomes are shown in the accompanying tabulation.

	Commercial Farm Operator Family Income	Nonfarm Family Income
1947..........	$4389	$4775
1948..........	4198	...
1949..........	3768	...
1950..........	3649	5232
1951..........	4224	5721
1952..........	4297	6013
1953..........	4291	6360
1954..........	3897	6297
1955..........	3868	...

These comparisons tell an interesting story. Average incomes of commercial farm operator families approached the nonfarm average more closely in 1947 than in any other year. But even in that bonanza year for agriculture, the average income of commercial farm operators fell noticeably short of the nonfarm average. And since 1947 average incomes of commercial farm operator families have declined in a persistent, but irregular, fashion. On the other hand, average incomes of all families in the nonfarm economy have increased in a persistent and regular fashion since 1947. So in this comparison, too, the farm income picture looks unattractive. The incomes of commercial farm operator families have slipped badly in the midst of unparalleled prosperity.

The Uncertainty Problem

The inefficient or nonoptimal use of farm resources resulting from commodity price uncertainty is not easy to document. No one has found a way to aggregate into one estimate or chart or empirical relation the inefficiencies in resource use that result from price uncertainty on some three million commercial farms across the nation. But, even if someone had, the estimate would probably not create too much excitement

[7] The procedure used to estimate the average incomes of commercial farm operator families by years is presented in Appendix Table 1.

24

because (1) such a measure, unlike personal income, would fall outside the experience of most men and (2) the implications of such a measure would be of primary importance for society as a whole, not for any group in particular.

Inefficiencies that result from price uncertainty are nevertheless widespread in agriculture and they serve to reduce the total production of *wanted* farm products. In this sense a problem exists. But it is a problem in which the layman generally finds it difficult to generate interest. In many respects it is like the problem of the common cold: everyone suffers from the common cold and the productive efficiency and personal well-being of each of us is decreased as a result, but most people don't worry unduly about colds — and there exist only a few wild estimates about the debilitating effects of the omnipresent cold.

The resource-use problems in agriculture arising out of price uncertainty can be illustrated, if not quantified. And that will be the procedure here; illustrations of the kinds of resource-use problems that arise out of price uncertainty in American agriculture will be presented. Let us first consider the problem of achieving a desirable pattern of resource use *over time in the production of a single commodity* (i.e., the production of an orderly supply of a commodity over time). This problem assumes a pure and almost beautiful form in the case of potatoes. The hog and beef cycles, and the in-and-out pattern of production for eggs and numerous vegetable crops, are other examples.

Variations in the prices and production of potatoes for the periods 1922–42 and 1950–56 are presented in Figure 5 (the period 1943–49 is omitted, for this is the period of effective price supports for potatoes). The inverse relationship between prices and production that emerges in Figure 5 suggests that potato producers have, over the years, based their price expectations (hence their planting decisions) upon prices received in the recent past (probably on prices received during the past one or two years). Large plantings made in response to high prices and in the expectation of high prices have resulted in an expanded output and low prices in the following year, which in turn has led to small plantings and high prices. The cycle has been particularly vicious because elasticity of the demand for potatoes is exceedingly low — meaning that relatively small acreage adjustments have resulted in relatively wide price swings.

The function of price as a connecting link between potato producers

25

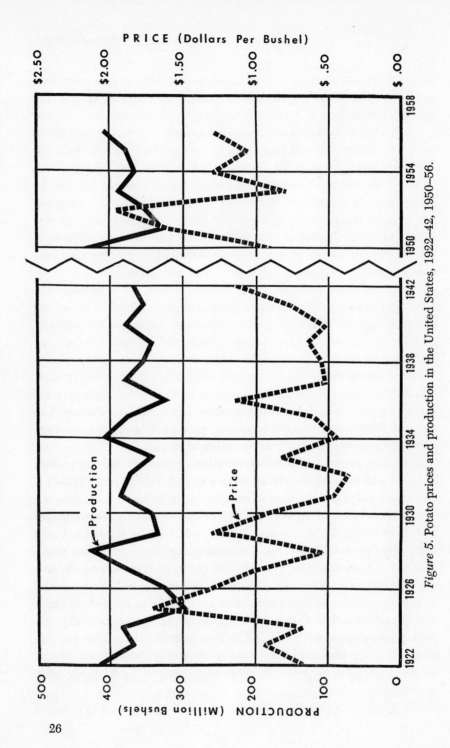

Figure 5. Potato prices and production in the United States, 1922–42, 1950–56.

26

and consumers has been seriously impaired in the free market. Individual producers, accustomed to thinking that high prices mean that more should be produced, and vice versa, have not received an accurate signal from the market. Whatever signal the consumer may have been sending, regarding the amount of potatoes that he wanted, that signal has been obscured by the violent price fluctuations resulting from the inflexibility of his demand for potatoes at any particular time.

In any given period the consumer has wanted a certain quantity of potatoes, largely irrespective of price. Instead, he has been offered quantities that varied widely from one year to the next, and, in consequence, he has paid more for his potatoes over a period of time than he would have had to pay for the same quantity if the year-to-year fluctuations had been less. The producer looking to the market for his signal has been repeatedly confounded by the signal, and as a result has been made increasingly conscious of the hazardous nature of potato production. His actual and expected costs have, therefore, been higher than they need to have been, and the workings of the cobweb mechanism have made for inefficiency.[8]

Let us consider next the problem of achieving a desirable pattern of resource use among commodities during a given period when commodity prices are uncertain. This problem can be illustrated with the aid of a hypothetical farm in a series of hypothetical price situations. The hypothetical, but nonetheless representative, farm is a cash grain farm in the Red River Valley of the North with three enterprise alternatives: wheat, barley, and flax (taking a case involving no livestock operations simplifies the presentation considerably and in no way invalidates the general conclusions). This cash grain farm, representative of the area, is 400 acres in size, of which 60 acres are regularly fallowed. This is a family farm, meaning that most of the labor employed is supplied by the farm family; but some custom work is contracted from time to time.

The assumed "actual" prices for wheat, barley, and flax are indicated opposite situation 1 in Table 2 (actually these are average prices for the period 1930–39, adjusted to 1950 levels). The acreages indicated for situation 1 represent the profit-maximizing, cost-minimizing combination of enterprises for the combination of prices given under situation

[8] The cobweb mechanism will be explained and then used as an explanation of commodity price behavior in Chapter 4.

1.[9] To get this illustration started we shall assume that this farmer some-how knew what prices were going to be in year one (i.e., he knew with certainty the combination of prices in situation 1), and he allocated his productive resources in an optimum fashion (i.e., as indicated by the number of acres devoted to each crop in situation 1).

Table 2. Price Combinations and Resource Use Patterns for a Hypothetical Cash Grain Farm, Kittson County, Red River Valley, Minnesota

Price Situation	Commodity Combination	Price Combination	Acres of Land Used
Situation 1:	Wheat	$2.08	170
"Actual" prices	Barley	1.28	100
in year one	Flax	3.18	70
Situation 2:	Wheat	2.08	170
"Expected" prices	Barley	1.28	88
in year two	Flax	3.85	82
Situation 3:	Wheat	2.08	170
"Realized" prices	Barley	1.50	170
in year two	Flax	3.18	0

This representative farmer does not, however, expect prices to remain the same in year two. He has a hunch — perhaps from reading some U.S. Department of Agriculture outlook information, or perhaps from talking to a local merchant — that the price of flax will increase to around $3.85 in year two. So he shifts some resources around at planting time in year two, increasing his production of flax and decreasing his production of barley in anticipation of higher flax prices. The profit-maximizing, cost-minimizing combination of enterprises consistent with this farmer's anticipated prices in year two is given opposite situation 2 in Table 2. But this farmer's price expectations are not realized: *he was wrong.* The price of flax held constant but the price of barley rose — perhaps because too many farmers shifted out of barley. In any event, the combination of enterprises selected by this farmer, as indicated by the acre allocations under situation 2 *is not optimum for the combination of prices* that he "realized" under situation 3. The prices "realized" in year two call for an increase in the acreage of barley over year one, and no flax production.

[9] This combination of enterprises, and others that follow, were derived by linear programming methods.

how many farmers drop out of a product because of prices anticipation lowers.

A set of price expectations for year two led this farmer astray; he did not allocate his resources optimally in year two *because his realized prices turned out to be different from his expected planning prices.* Price uncertainty in this situation led to production inefficiency. Now multiply this illustration by some three million commercial farms and duplicate it year after year, and the magnitude of this resource-use problem arising out of commodity price uncertainty begins to emerge.

Price-Income Instability — The Norm for Agriculture

It is abundantly clear that farm prices are not stable, certain things. As the farmer sees them and feels them, they gyrate in a most confusing manner. With a little analysis some of this confusion can be eliminated; a little analysis suggests that there are really two kinds of farm price variability: (1) movements in the level of farm prices and (2) year-to-year variations in farm commodity prices around the moving farm price level. But this analysis does not wash price variability out of the picture; rather it sharpens the picture and brings into focus the two different forms of variability involved.

It makes clear, first, that the level of farm prices moves in broad and dramatic sweeps, that these wide sweeps date back to the Civil War and before, and that the amplitude and frequency of those sweeps have intensified since World War I, but that no cyclical, or periodic, behavior is to be found in them. *In sum, wide and irregular swings in the farm price level are the norm.*

It makes clear, second, that all commodity prices tend to follow the same general and tortuous path, but that individual commodity prices bob around the unfolding level in an irregular and jerky fashion, and that farm commodities vary considerably with respect to the degree of year-to-year variability exhibited by them. *In sum, a continuum of commodity price variability, from almost none to extreme, around the moving farm price level is the norm.*

Now if farmers and consumers, and businessmen as well, enjoy price variability, no problem or problems can be said to exist. In this unlikely event farmers and consumers have found a heaven on earth, for in agriculture they find the ultimate in price variability. But it has been argued here that a serious economic problem grows out of each of the two forms of price variability isolated. Wide fluctuations in the farm price level lead to a general and overriding income consequence, which

29

in periods of declining prices constitutes a problem. The good and the bad farmers suffer when all farm prices come tumbling down; and when these periods are prolonged, farm business failure becomes widespread. This is the problem that terrifies farm people; this is the problem that has forced agriculture into politics, and keeps it there.

Price uncertainty resulting from irregular year-to-year commodity price variations around the moving farm price level gives rise to a less terrifying problem than the income problem, but a more general one. Because of price uncertainty — because realized prices rarely turn out to be the same as expected, planning prices — resource combinations are rarely optimum. This chronic problem goes on and on annoying producers, and reducing by some unknown amount the total satisfaction of consumers.

If it is conceded that the income problem and the uncertainty problem are real problems (and who would want to argue that they are not?), then these problems too are the norm for agriculture. They do not arise out of transitory phenomena; they are the logical and continuing consequences of chronic price instability in agriculture.

PART II

An Analysis of Farm Price
Behavior

3

Price Level Fluctuations

We know that the farm price level moves through time in wide and dramatic swings. We know also that these swings tend to be more frequent and of greater amplitude than those for the nonfarm sector. But why? Why do we get these wide and irregular fluctuations in the farm price level? This is the question to which this chapter is addressed.

As we shall see, the explanation is to be found in the unique behavior of consumers on the one hand, and of producers on family farms on the other. But behavior with respect to what, that is the question. A single food item, or all food, by the consumer? A single enterprise, or total production of the farm, by the farmer? The unit of inquiry is all important here. And the failure to select and employ a unit of inquiry which can and properly does deal with the problem under consideration (i.e., fluctuations in the level of farm prices) has led many an analyst astray.

To illustrate, a consumer behaves very differently with respect to a single food item, such as pork chops, than he does with respect to all meat, or with respect to all food. If the price of pork chops rises relative to other food items, the consumer typically cuts back his consumption of pork chops and substitutes other food items — beef or poultry, for example — for the now more expensive pork chops. The composition of the consumer's food basket changes, but the total quantity of meat, or of all food, consumed changes very little.

But let the prices of all food items rise and what does the consumer do? He perhaps reduces his consumption of all foods modestly by reason of the fact that he is now a poorer man — his real income has declined as the result of increased food prices. *But he does not substitute nonfood*

33

items for food, because the aggregate food does not have a close, or generally accepted, substitute.

The consumer thus varies his consumption of single food items (pork chops, tomatoes, eggs, peaches) as the prices of those items vary, but this he cannot do with respect to all food. The substitutional possibilities for the consumer have changed importantly in moving from the single item to the whole: pork chops have many food substitutes; all food, practically none. And to reason that a consumer will curtail his consumption of total food with an increase in all food prices, because he behaves this way with respect to a single food item, is to reason falsely. This is the celebrated *fallacy of composition* where the analyst falsely reasons that what is true for the part is necessarily true for the whole.

Now to turn this argument around, if we want to develop an explanation of the fluctuations in all food, or farm, prices (i.e., the level of farm prices), we cannot do this by concentrating on single commodities. The single commodity has substitutional possibilities on the consumption side and on the production side that are not open to food in the aggregate.[1] The aggregate food has few close substitutes on either the consumption or production side; the single commodity many. Thus if our price variable is the *level of food prices,* the quantity variable must be the aggregate food, if the unit of inquiry is to be meaningful and consistent. In other words, the analysis of this chapter will be conducted in aggregative terms — an aggregative analysis to cope with an aggregative problem.

The Aggregate Demand for Food

CONSUMPTION BEHAVIOR

The composition of the average American's diet has changed markedly over the past fifty years. The place of potatoes and cereals in the diet has declined steadily, the place of fruits and vegetables has increased steadily, and the consumption of most animal products increased noticeably during and immediately following World War II. *But over-all food consumption by the average consumer has changed but little since 1910.* In pounds of food consumed, it has changed almost not at all; per capita

[1] Since the aggregate food, fiber, and tobacco makes little sense on the consumption side, and since limiting the aggregate to food on the production side does not seriously impair the analysis (food production comprises about 85 per cent of total agricultural production), we shall hereafter in this chapter work with the aggregate food, and assume that the analysis is representative of agriculture as a whole.

food consumption stood at 1594 pounds per year in 1910 and it stood at 1531 pounds in 1954.

Pounds of food consumed is not, however, a good measure of food consumption. It fails to take into account shifts in the composition of the diet over the years — shifts from low-resource-using foods such as potatoes and cereals to high-resource-using foods such as animal products. The index of per capita food consumption[2] does, however, take these shifts into account — the index of per capita food consumption rises, for example, as a pound of high-priced beef steak is substituted for a pound of inexpensive wheat flour, and conversely. And we see from Figure 6 that the index holds almost constant from 1910 to 1937; it thrusts upward some 15 per cent between 1937 and 1946; and it fails to increase since 1946.

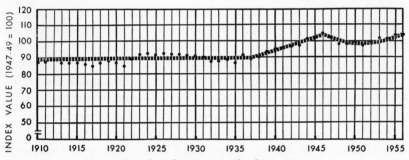

Figure 6. Index of per capita food consumption
in the United States, 1910–56.

Between 1910 and 1937, decreases in cereal and potato consumption by the average consumer were just about offset by increases in fruit and vegetable consumption, so that the index of per capita food consumption holds constant. Between 1937 and 1946, increases in animal product consumption expanded total food consumption for the average consumer for the first and only time during the extended period 1910–56. And since 1946 the average consumer has failed to increase his consumption of total food. He has consumed many more services associated with food items since 1946, and many more conveniences built into those

[2] This is a price-weighted index which weights food items into the index in accordance with market prices for the base period. See *Consumption of Food in the United States, 1909–52,* U.S.D.A. Agr. Handbook No. 62, September 1953, pp. 157–159 for a discussion of the index.

food items, but he has not upped his acquisitions of farm food products.

What we observe, then, is that over the years consumers slowly change their food habits. And once in a blue moon, as during and immediately following World War II when personal incomes skyrocketed, consumers change the composition of their diets radically. But in the main, consumers go along day after day, week after week, and month after month demanding and purchasing about the same kinds of the same quantities of foods. The average consumer does not want two meals a day when the prices of all foods rise, and he does not want four meals when the prices of all foods decline. He wants about the same quantities of the same kinds of foods regardless of price. He may change the composition of his diet somewhat as his income changes — substituting animal products for cereals and potatoes as he moves up the income ladder. But at any particular level of income, and in any particular cultural setting, the total quantity of farm food products purchased by the consumer changes very little with changes in the level of food prices.

At first blush this may seem strange. But it is strange only in terms of our experience with particular food items — a particular cut of meat, or a variety of apples. Further reflection on the constancy of food habits with respect to categories of foods (e.g., all meats or all fruits) and the compelling aspects of hunger make the sort of consumer behavior described above seem entirely reasonable. The consumer wants, and feels that he must have, three meals (or however many he regularly eats) each day. These food demands are compelling for him. And, as we shall see, these compelling demands have important implications for consumers themselves, and for the agricultural industry.

THE CONCEPT OF AGGREGATE DEMAND

The ideas under consideration here can be expressed in a rigorous form regularly employed by economists, namely, the demand relation. The demand relation of a consumer for a single commodity describes the quantities of that commodity that the consumer stands ready to take at varying prices, when all other influencing factors — consumer incomes, tastes and preferences, and prices of substitutes — hold constant. Market demand for a commodity is the summation of individual consumer demands for that commodity.

The concept *aggregate demand for food* describes the quantities of total food that all consumers stand ready to take at varying levels of food prices, when all other influencing factors are held constant. (Often the aggregate demand relation for food is expressed in terms of the average consumer rather than the total population; this construction does not change the concept since the quantity variable is the total food consumption of the average consumer.) This is a relationship of great importance, for once it is known we can predict the total quantity of food that will be purchased by consumers at different levels of food prices. And once we can do this for some given level and pattern of personal incomes and tastes and preferences in the United States, we can say how much food prices must fall to move some additional quantity of food into consumption, or the converse.

Since we already know something about consumer behavior with respect to the aggregate food, we also know something about the nature (i.e., the price elasticity) of the aggregate demand for food. The aggregate demand for food is severely inelastic — meaning that a large percentage change in price is associated with a small percentage change in the quantity taken. In other words, the aggregate demand for food states that consumers increase their takings of total food only modestly with a large decline in food prices, and decrease their takings of total food only modestly with a large increase in food prices. This we knew already, but the demand relation states this relationship precisely, and more importantly it enables us to measure the relationship involved.

MEASURES OF THE AGGREGATE DEMAND FOR FOOD

In recent years numerous estimates of the aggregate demand for food have been made.[3] Although each estimate has its limitations and difficulties, there is a general consensus that the elasticity of demand for all food at retail for the interwar period was around —.25. This measure of elasticity may be interpreted as follows: the total quantity of food purchased at retail, as measured by the index of per capita food consumption, decreases 2.5 per cent with a 10 per cent increase in retail food prices. In short, the aggregate demand for food was highly inelastic during the interwar period.

There are logical reasons for believing that the aggregate demand for food has become more inelastic in the post–World Year II period.

[3] For a brief summary of these estimates, see Table 11–1 in T. W. Schultz's *Economic Organization of Agriculture* (New York: McGraw-Hill, 1953), p. 188.

Rising real incomes and widespread nutritional education, both experienced in the post–World War II period, should lead to greater inelasticity in the demand for food. The income argument runs as follows: the proportion of income allocated to food declines with rising real incomes, and where the proportion of income allocated to an item of expenditure declines, the income effect to a consumer of a change in the price of that item becomes proportionately less. A price change on a minor item in the budget, for example, can have little effect on the real income of the consumer and hence can have little effect on the quantity of the item demanded. In other words, the over-all category food (i.e., farm food products) is becoming more and more like safety pins in the consumer's budget, and the place of safety pins in the consumer's budget is so small that he does not care whether a package costs 5 cents or 10 cents.

In the case of nutrition, it may be argued that nutritional education causes people to view different food groups somewhat as they do medicine; the consumer must have, he feels, so many pounds, or units, of each food group to stay healthy. Given the cultural setting, with an accepted structure of food habits and preferences, nutritional education reinforces the will of the consumer to acquire so many units of each major food group regardless of price.

So we have reason to believe that the aggregate demand for food is becoming more inelastic, and continuous estimating work bears out this hypothesis. Three different estimates of the aggregate demand for food made by the author for progressively later periods, and by essentially the same methods, yield the following results:

Period	Elasticity at Points of Means
1922–41	−.31
1929–42, 1947–49	−.23
1929–42, 1947–56	−.10

These estimates support the hypothesis that the aggregate demand relation for food, which was severely inelastic during the interwar period, is becoming progressively more inelastic. The last estimate of −0.1 is very low indeed. It says that per capita food consumption will increase only 1 per cent with a 10 per cent decrease in the retail level of food prices.

The demand relation for the last estimate of price elasticity is presented graphically in Figure 7.[4] It will be noted that the demand curve DD in Figure 7 (a straight line on arithmetic paper) fits the annual price-quantity points closely. In other words, this demand relation does a good job of explaining changes in per capita food consumption in terms of changes in retail food prices, where the influences of income and time are removed from the analysis. It should be noted further, however, that the price elasticity estimate at the point of means, $E = -0.1$, falls in between the interwar and postwar periods, and reporting the elasticity at that point on the curve is somewhat meaningless. At a price level of 110 on the index of retail prices the elasticity estimate is $E = -0.16$.[5] Thus, we may conclude that the elasticity of demand for all food at the 1950–55 level of retail food prices is somewhere between -0.15 and -0.2.

The demand relation DD portrayed in Figure 7 is an average relation — for the average consumer and for the average income and trend for the period 1929–42 and 1947–56. The statistical analysis removed the influences of changes in income, and, it is hoped, changes in tastes and preferences, through the trend factor, to enable us to estimate an aggregate demand relation for food for *the average consumer* for the period in question. But it would be wrong to visualize the aggregate demand relation for food *for the nation* as holding constant over this eventful period.

The latter relation was expanding over the period for two principal reasons. First, rising real incomes caused the average consumer to demand more total food — not more pounds, but more farm resources — during this period. This was the period in which the average consumer made important changes in the composition of his diet — substituting high-resource-using animal products for low-resource-using farm commodities. Second, the number of average consumers greatly increased during this period; the number of mouths to be fed in the United States increased by 45 million between 1929 and 1956. Thus, the aggregate demand relation for food is not a static thing; it is an expanding thing — expanding through time at a relentless but uneven pace. Population

[4] The data, regression equation, and other relevant statistical measures of this demand analysis are to be found in Appendix Table 2. The regression line DD in Figure 7 minimizes the sum of the squares of the horizontal deviations. The yearly observations in Figure 7 are plotted from columns 1 and 5 of Appendix Table 2.

[5] It is the property of a straight line on arithmetic paper that the measure of elasticity changes at every point along it: rising going up the curve and declining coming down it.

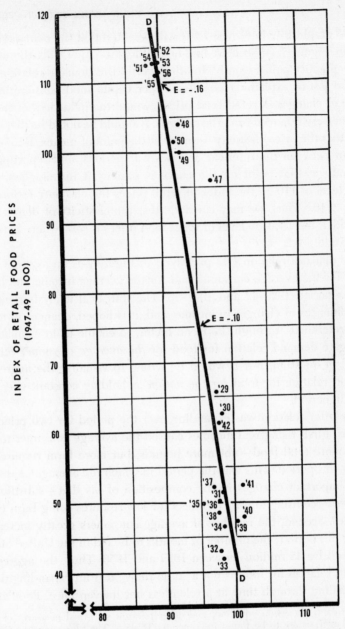

Figure 7. The aggregate demand curve for food, 1929–42, 1947–56. The
variable, index of per capita food consumption, is adjusted
for changes in income and trend.

growth is the powerful and persistent shifter of the relation, income change the less important and sporadic shifter.

IMPLICATIONS FOR AGRICULTURE

Tremendous implications flow from the aggregate demand relation described above. It is probably correct to say that the severely inelastic aggregate demand relation for food, growing out of the regular eating habits of consumers, and becoming increasingly inelastic over time, makes agriculture the unique industry that it is and gives agriculture a feast and famine quality of dubious worth. It is this severe inelasticity of demand that forces farm prices to fluctuate in the extreme, and in turn creates a general income problem in agriculture.

Other economic forces contribute to this general income problem, as we shall see. But in this severely inelastic demand relation for aggregate food we encounter one of the key causative elements of the income problem in agriculture.

To illustrate, and assuming the elasticity of demand to be $E = -.2$, retail food prices must fall 10 per cent to move 2 per cent more food into consumption. But does this mean that farm prices will fall only 10 per cent? The answer is no. Farm prices must fall in the neighborhood of 25 per cent to move 2 per cent more food into consumption. This greater percentage change in prices at the farm level results from the unresponsiveness of the farm marketing system. The full shock of a change in food prices at retail is absorbed by farm prices; the various marketing charges for handling, storing, transporting, and processing are virtually unaffected in the short run by retail price changes. And where the marketing system absorbs some 60 per cent of the consumer's food dollar, it follows that a price change that amounts to 10 per cent at retail, amounts to a 25 per cent change at the farm level. In other words, a 10 cent decline on $1.00 amounts to a 10 per cent decline, but a 10 cent decline on 40 cents amounts to a 25 per cent decline. And this is just about what we have in agriculture.

This price-quantity relation at the farm level, too, can be expressed in terms of elasticity of demand. The elasticity of demand for all food at the farm level is $-.08$. Other things being equal (assuming no change in personal incomes, tastes and preferences, or marketing margins), a 2 per cent decline in the over-all amount of food products offered on the market will drive farm prices up by 25 per cent, and a 2 per cent increase in the amount offered will drive prices down by 25 per cent. The farmer is truly at the crack end of the whip.

The income consequences of this low demand elasicity are that a fall in prices received by farmers greatly reduces cash receipts, and an increase in prices received greatly increases cash receipts. The following arithmetic example, constructed to yield a price elasticity of — .08 at the farm level, illustrates the gross income consequences involved:

			Cash
Price	*Quantity*		*Receipts*
125	×	98	=	12,250
100	×	100	=	10,000
75	×	102	=	7,650

Where the elasticity of demand for all food at the farm level equals —.08, gross farm income fluctuates almost as widely as farm prices do. And those price level fluctuations are wide indeed.

Consumer behavior with respect to the aggregate category food, which results in a low price elasticity at retail, and the large and unresponsive marketing changes, which result in an even lower price elasticity at the farm level, thus have important implications for agriculture. These considerations explain in large measure the extreme price and income level fluctuations to be found in agriculture.

The Aggregate Supply of Food

By the term *supply relation,* or *supply curve,* economists typically have in mind how the quantity of a *product* offered for sale varies, as its price varies relative to other product prices, *for some given time period and for a given state of the arts, or technology.*[6] The concept is used to describe how the quantity of a commodity offered on the market varies by reason of resources flowing into, or out of, the enterprises producing the commodity, as the price of the commodity varies relative to other, substitute, commodities. Implicit in the concept are the notions (1) that one or more factors may be varied in the production processes involved and (2) that these factors are substitutable among enterprises, firms, and industries (i.e., factors can in

---

[6] This section is adapted from the article "Conceptualizing the Supply Relation in Agriculture" by Willard W. Cochrane, *Journal of Farm Economics,* Proceedings Number, December 1955.

practice vary, where they are technically variable). Explicit is the notion that the concept is net, relating quantity supplied to price, where all other influencing conditions are held constant (for example, technological advance). The concept of supply is a rigorous one: reversible and timeless as regards dated time. It finds a useful and meaningful role in economic analysis in the way of explaining price formation in a *market*; when the rigorous concept of supply is related to an equally rigorous concept of demand an explanation of market price emerges.

THE SUPPLY RELATION FOR THE FARM FIRM

The question to be answered here is: How does the concept of supply change, as the unit of inquiry changes from that of the commodity to that of the farm firm? In the first place, the basic definition does not change. The economist is still concerned with describing how the quantity offered for sale varies as price varies, for some given time period and as all other influencing conditions are held constant. But now his concern is with the quantity offered for sale by the firm, not by the suppliers of one commodity. And the typical farm firm is a multiple enterprise unit producing several different commodities. Thus, the supply relation for the multiple enterprise firm must describe how the *aggregate* of commodities produced and offered for sale varies as the prices of those commodities vary.

In this context, the variable *price* converts into an average, or level, of prices, in order to deal with several prices, and the variable *quantity* converts into an index number of quantity in order to deal with several different commodities. The concept of a supply relation for the firm is thus complicated by the index number problem, but the concept is in no wise invalidated. On the contrary, it is conceptually possible, and just as important, to describe the supply relation involving the aggregate output of a farm as it is to describe a single commodity relation.

Most economists agree that the short-run supply relation for the typical farm firm is highly inelastic. They may skirmish among themselves with respect to just how inelastic this relation may be, but not about the general proposition. This means that the aggregate output of the farm firm changes very little with a rise or fall in the level of prices for the commodities involved although, of course, the composition

43

of the aggregate may change importantly. This inelasticity of aggregate output results from a number of interrelated and interacting causes.

First, on family farms family labor, land, and many forms of capital are treated as fixed-cost inputs in the short run; in the going concern of the family farm the cost of these inputs does not change appreciably whether they are used or not, hence they are employed fully.

Second, in periods of falling product prices farm labor, land, and sunk capital lack alternatives; hence the returns to these resources fall along with the prices of the products which they produce, and they continue to be employed on the same farms. In periods of rising product prices land and labor resources cannot be increased on each farm by operators bidding against one another for those resources already employed on farms. And land and labor do not easily flow back and forth across the farm-nonfarm line in response to factor prices. In short, the supply relation for many farm resources is highly inelastic.

Third, the returns attributable to productive efforts of such factors as tractors and combines, dairy cows and breeding stock, and orchards and feed grains (i.e., the marginal value products of these factors) may vary over a wide range, as the prices of the products they produce vary widely, without there being an incentive for the farmer to employ more or fewer of these factor inputs. This is the case because, even though returns attributable to these factors fluctuate widely, the returns do not rise above the acquisition costs of the factors on the high side, or fall below the salvage values of the factors on the low side.[7]

Fourth, to some degree farmers view their occupation as a way of life as well as a business; they do not always respond readily to price-income stimuli. For all of these reasons the productive resources on family farms tend to remain fixed in, and fully employed on, those farms over the short run. Hence the total output of each farm varies only modestly with a change in the level of prices (i.e., the supply relation of the firm tends to be severely inelastic).

To illustrate this phenomenon of sustained output, let us visualize the operation of a multiple-enterprise family farm involving corn, hogs, dairy, soybeans, and eggs. Now let the price of soybeans fall relative

[7] This novel and plausible explanation for the fixity of inputs in agriculture was presented by Glenn Johnson at the North Central Farm Management Research Committee Conference, Chicago, March 18–21, 1957, in a paper entitled "Some Facts and Notions about the Supply Function for Agriculture — Their Relationship to Agricultural Problems and Prosperity in the Next Two Decades."

to the other commodity prices; in this event the operator will be inclined to reduce his production of soybeans. But the acres taken out of soybeans will not remain idle; they will go into more corn or oats or hay. The increased supply of feed is converted into more eggs, dairy products, or hogs, and the total output of the farm measured in terms of a price-weighted index holds approximately constant or perhaps declines modestly. Or let the prices of all five products fall proportionately. In this case there will be no shifting of resources among enterprises, but neither will there be a contraction in total output. For the combination of reasons recounted above, the resources of the farm remain fully employed and output is maintained.

THE AGGREGATE SUPPLY RELATION FOR THE NATION

The aggregate supply relation for the nation at the farm level is simply the summation of individual firm supply relations. And since the typical supply relation for farm firms is severely inelastic, it must follow that the aggregate supply relation for the nation is also severely inelastic. Within the national aggregate, supply adjustments take place among commodities in accordance with individual commodity supply elasticities (as we shall see in Chapter 4), but over all, and in the short run, output is maintained. The aggregate supply of farm products for the nation changes little, if at all, with changes in the farm price level.

This generalization is consistent with information concerning the over-all employment of resources in agriculture. The index of total inputs in agriculture changes only modestly from year to year; during the period 1920 to 1950 the index moves within the narrow range of 100 to 110 and shows no discernible trend. T. W. Schultz summarizes this stability in the use of inputs as follows: "The quantity of inputs committed to farm production from one year to the next is the most stable economic variable in agriculture. It is doubtful that one could find another major variable in the entire economy that is as steady. . . ."[8] The total output of agriculture may vary from other causes — for example, from a serious drought, or the widespread adoption of the gasoline engine — but not from a purposive expansion or contraction of total resources employed. Over the years the increased employment of capital has just about offset the decreased employment of labor to hold constant the total inputs committed to agricultural production.

[8] *The Economic Organization of Agriculture* (New York: McGraw-Hill, 1953), p. 210.

45

THE KEY ROLE OF TECHNOLOGICAL ADVANCE

To this point, the role of technological advance on farms has been ignored, or assumed away, in order that we could conceptualize the various supply relations.[9] But to ignore the role of technological advance is to ignore the principal way in which the total output of agriculture has expanded since 1900 and the almost exclusive way it has expanded since 1920. Total inputs employed in American agriculture have held almost constant since 1920, but total production has not. The trend of total production has been upward at a little over 1 per cent per year since 1920. This rate of increase must be ascribed to technological advance; there is nothing else to ascribe it to. This inference does not seem unreasonable, however, in light of what we all know has been occurring on farms. Farm operators generally have adopted a wide range of new and improved production methods: improved plant varieties, improved breeds of livestock, improved sanitation practices, the general purpose tractor and endless machine hookups, new methods of insect and pest control, supplementary irrigation, new views on fertilizer application, improved feeding practices, and so on.

The modern farmer rarely adds, or varies, identical units of capital inputs; typically he moves from one resource mix in one planning period to a new and improved resource mix involving new practices and new technologies in the next planning period. Generally a new resource mix, involving a new and more productive production plan, entails an additional cash outlay to acquire some new capital good, but not always. The key point to bear in mind is that present-day farm operators have come to regard the adoption of new and improved production methods as a regular thing; they expect to make such adoptions year after year. Thus, technological advance is the dynamic force in agriculture, being involved in almost all production adjustments and explaining net increases in output on individual farms and in the aggregate.

Although a technological advance by definition involves an increase in output per unit of input, or a decrease in unit costs, and thus, other things being equal, an advance must have the effect of increasing net farm returns, it does not follow that the adoption of new technologies on farms always occurs steadily and easily. In the first place, the new technologies must be there to be adopted, and farmers must know about

[9] Technological advance may be defined as follows: an increase in output per unit of input resulting from a new organization, or configuration, of inputs where a new and more productive production function is involved.

46

them. Once this was the important barrier to farm technological advance, but not today. The vast sums spent by public and private agencies on research into new methods and practices and in carrying these new methods and practices out to farmers has broken down this pre-twentieth-century barrier. But some other problems do remain.

The adoption of a new or improved production technique most often requires an additional investment in some new resource or input. This added investment requires, in turn, an additional cash outlay or financial commitment. Now when are farmers able and willing to make such investments? They are able when their asset positions are strong, and willing when the future does not look too risky. Thus, the financial position of farmers and the riskiness of the enterprise can and does influence the rate of adoption of new and improved technologies. Typically the rate of adoption will be fast in good times when expectations are bright and asset positions are good, and slow in hard times when expectations are dim and asset positions are impaired.

In terms of the aggregate supply relations discussed above, both for single firms and nationally, this means that those relations have not been holding constant. Under the force of technological advance they have moved to the right in an expanding action. As output per unit of input has increased, the typical farm firm stands ready to offer more products for sale at any particular price; thus we say that the supply curve, by commodities and in the aggregate, has shifted to the right.

It is probably not correct to visualize the aggregate supply relation of farm food products moving to the right over the past several decades at an even pace, however. The aggregate supply relation has expanded in a hopping or skipping action. This is true because the rate of technological advance has not been steady. And since the rate of technological advance over the years has not been steady, the rate of increase in production efficiency growing out of that technological advance has not been steady.

Figure 8 makes this clear. Over-all efficiency in agriculture did not increase between 1910 and 1920; the trend line of efficiency holds constant over this period — perhaps the nonavailability of important new technologies explains this period. An upward thrust in efficiency does, however, manifest itself in the period 1921–24; this thrust is probably associated with the widespread adoption of the tractor and the gasoline engine. The 1921–24 period is followed by a long quiescent span of

47

years, 1924–36, with no important gains in efficiency; this is a period of hard times for American agriculture — times not conducive to farm technological advance.

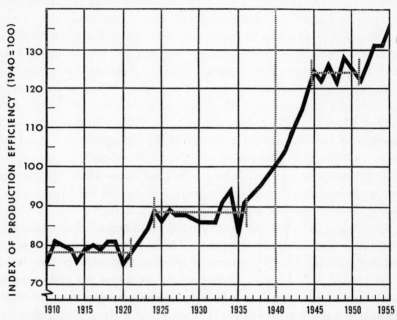

Figure 8. Changes in production efficiency in agriculture, 1910–55. The index of production efficiency is the index of farm marketing and home consumption divided by the index of total agricultural inputs multiplied by 100. The index from 1910 to 1940 includes all agricultural inputs; the index from 1940 to 1955 includes farm labor, land, buildings, fertilizer and lime, depreciation and interest charges, and operating expenses of machinery and equipment.

Next emerges that great period of technological advance in American agriculture, 1936–44, with spectacular gains in production efficiency. Finally, production efficiency levels off once again in the immediate post–World War II years, but in 1951 it begins its upward drive once more. The economic meaning of these spurts in technological advance, and therefore of production efficiency, must be that the aggregate supply relation jumped to the right in an expanding action during these spurts. And during periods of little or no gain in productive efficiency, the aggregate supply relation must have held fixed positions.

This general view of the relationship of technological advance to the aggregate supply relation is presented in Figure 9. In this figure, the

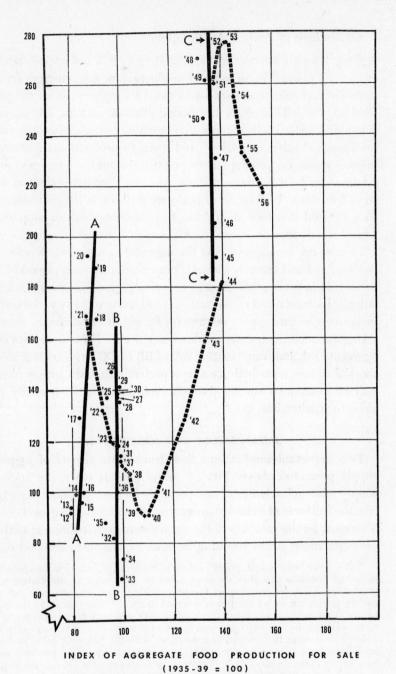

Figure 9. The aggregate supply curve for food.

49

aggregate supply relation for food, relating an index of responsible (i.e., causative) prices [10] to an index of production for sale, emerges for each period of technological quiescence: the AA supply curve for the period 1912–21, the BB curve for the period 1924–36 and the CC curve for the period 1944–51. In other words, in those periods when the rate of technological advance is slow, and gains in production efficiency are imperceptible, the price-quantity points trace out the aggregate supply relations for food for those periods. And the aggregate relations so derived turn out to be severely or perfectly inelastic as the previous analysis suggested that they should be; the empirical analysis supports the logical conclusions.

To sum up, we observe that the aggregate supply relation for food holds a fixed and severely inelastic position during each period of little or no gain in production efficiency. But in periods of widespread technological advance and rapid gains in production efficiency, the severely inelastic aggregate supply relation for food shifts, or drifts, to the right, taking up successively more productive positions. (The movement of the aggregate relation from position AA to BB to CC by years is traced by the dashed line; a perfectly, or almost perfectly, inelastic supply function may be envisioned cutting through each annual price-quantity point along the dashed line.)

IMPLICATIONS FOR AGRICULTURE

Two important implications flow from the concepts of aggregate supply presented above. First, in those periods when the aggregate supply relation holds a fixed and perfectly inelastic position (e.g., 1924–36), the full force of a change in demand shoots into a price level change. This must be the case where the aggregate supply relation is perfectly inelastic: rising prices resulting from an expansion in demand do not

[10] The term "responsible prices" refers to those prices which cause farmers to make the decisions that they do in planning for this year's, or the current year's, production. Thus, we may expect the responsible prices, in most cases, not to be current prices, but rather the prices received in some earlier period. In the case of annual crops, perhaps when last year's crops were sold; in the case of dairy or beef cattle, perhaps the two years previous to the year in question. The index of responsible prices used in this analysis is constructed with the following price leads: (1) lambs, chickens, hogs — average monthly prices from July of the previous year to June of the current year; (2) beef cattle — average price for the current year and previous year; (3) eggs — average price for the current year and previous year; (4) dairy products — average price for the current year and two previous years; (5) crops — average monthly price from July to December for the previous year.

induce an increase in the total quantity offered and hence do not give rise to a moderating influence on price itself; falling prices fail to induce a contraction in output and hence fail to put a brake on the falling prices. In these periods, which are sometimes short and sometimes long, the aggregate demand relation, as it expands and contracts, simply rides up and down a fixed and perfectly inelastic supply function. This unresponsive supply behavior in the aggregate thus helps to generate wide swings in the farm price level.

The second implication is less dramatic, but perhaps more profound. Even though the aggregate supply relation is perfectly inelastic, the aggregate output of agriculture has increased over the years — by some 90 per cent since 1914. But this increase in total output, at least since 1920, has not resulted from an increase in the total resources employed in agriculture at higher product prices. If this were the case, the aggregate supply relation in agriculture would slope upward and to the right; it would be positively inclined. The increases in total output that have occurred, have resulted from the employment of almost the same total quantity of resources (valued in constant prices), *but different and more productive resources* (i.e., from technological advance).

Thus it is wrong, as wrong can be, to conclude that a falling farm price level will reduce total farm output. The increases in total farm output that have occurred over the past thirty-five years have resulted from the adoption of cost-reducing production practices and, once adopted, those practices have not been abandoned with falling prices. Just as they served to maximize profits under good prices, they serve to minimize losses under low prices. The kind of output expansion experienced in American agriculture, *in the aggregate*, over the past thirty-five years is *nonreversible*. In periods of falling farm prices, sustained output is the norm for agriculture.

But the converse is not necessarily true. Rising farm prices and the expectation of continued rising prices can speed up the rate of farm technological advance, hence speed up the rate of aggregate output expansion, hence serve to shift the aggregate supply relation more rapidly. This follows from what we have already observed, namely, that most new techniques adopted on farms require additional capital inputs involving additional cash outlays or extended financial commitments. These additional cash outlays or financial commitments are easy to make, relatively speaking, in prosperous times, but difficult in hard times. Thus, farmers adopt those production practices in prosperous times that they know they should, because financially they can; but they fail to make those technological advances in hard times that they know they should, because sources of financing have dried up.

The explanation for changes in total farm output, or, more accurately, the explanation for changes in the rate of total output expansion, does not run in terms of variations in the employment of total farm resources; it runs in terms of speeding up and slowing down the rate of farm technological advance. Farm technological advance powers output expansion in American agriculture.

The Complete System

We now have the two necessary building blocks of a complete system for explaining farm price level fluctuations. First, we know what the aggregate demand relation for food is — we understand the concept; we know what it is like — we have measures of its elasticity; we know why it behaves as it does — we know what causes it to shift; and we appreciate its implications — we know what it can do. Second, we know what the aggregate supply relation for food is — we understand the concept; we know what it is like — we have measures of its elasticity; we know why it behaves as it does — we know what causes it to shift; and we appreciate its implications — we know what it can do. It is a relatively simple matter, then, to relate the aggregate supply and demand relations for food in an illustrative model for explaining price level movements. And this we shall do.

AN ILLUSTRATIVE MODEL FOR THE 1950s

In Figure 10 we have a stripped down, highly simplified model which may be used to illustrate or explain the nature of price level movements for all farm food products as of the 1950s. The supply relation is perfectly inelastic as the logical and empirical analyses suggest is the case. The elasticity of demand at the point of departure for this analysis (price level = 100, total quantity = 100) is —.08, or the estimate deduced earlier as the price elasticity of aggregate demand at the farm level. Finally, it should be noted that this is a farm level model, and the price level solutions generated by it are for food products at the farm level.

Even a cursory glance at this model suggests one thing and one thing only: *any small change in demand, or supply, must give rise to a large*

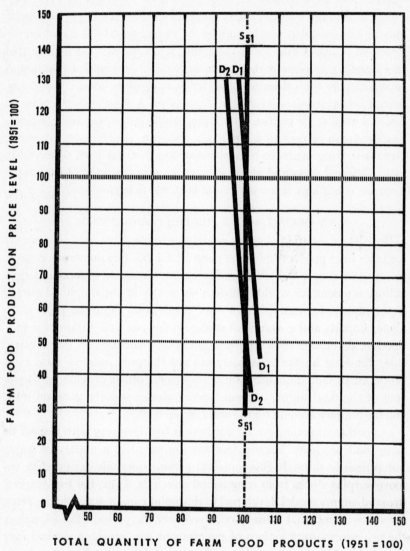

Figure 10. Farm food price level generating model:
illustrative model of the 1950s.

change in the farm price level. More specifically, a 4 per cent contraction in demand, a movement in demand from D_1 to D_2 in Figure 10, results in a 50 per cent decline in farm prices. This is a big price decline but, if this model properly represents the aggregate demand-supply structure of agriculture as of the 1950s, it is a price level decline that could easily take place within a year or two in a *free market situation.* A contraction in total demand of 4 per cent or more would result, say, from a moderate-sized economic depression. A 4 per cent increase in demand would, of course, have comparable price-enhancing effects; similarly with respect to a 4 per cent increase, or decrease, in supply. Here is striking evidence of a phenomenon that has been observed in many different ways and places in recent years: the finest of lines separates the conditions of too much and too little in agriculture.

A WORKING MODEL FOR THE PERIOD 1951-55

Now let us use the foregoing model to explain price level movements for farm food products over the period 1951-55. For numerous reasons this is not a simple task. First and foremost, the world of food and agriculture is a complex world that does not neatly fit our simplified model. Total supply, for example, does not result from domestic production alone; imports and government storage policy, as well as domestic production, determine total supply in any one year. And on the demand side, domestic human consumers are not the only users of farm food products. In fact, domestic human consumers utilize only about 64 per cent of the total supply of farm food products; exports, nonfood uses, and the military account for the other 36 per cent.

In another direction, we do not have a free economy with respect to farm food products. Farm prices are supported in a variety of ways, but primarily through governmental action programs designed to remove surplus stocks from commercial channels. Thus, the free-market, demand-supply model developed to this point cannot generate the price level movements that actually occurred over the period 1951-55, unless the price-supporting actions of government are somehow worked into the model. This we do in the working model presented in Figure 11, along with the interjection of certain heroic assumptions, as well as some patchwork to take account of certain loose ends. And having done this, we obtain a model that works tolerably well.

The supply curve $S_{51} S_{51}$ in Figure 11 represents the total supply of

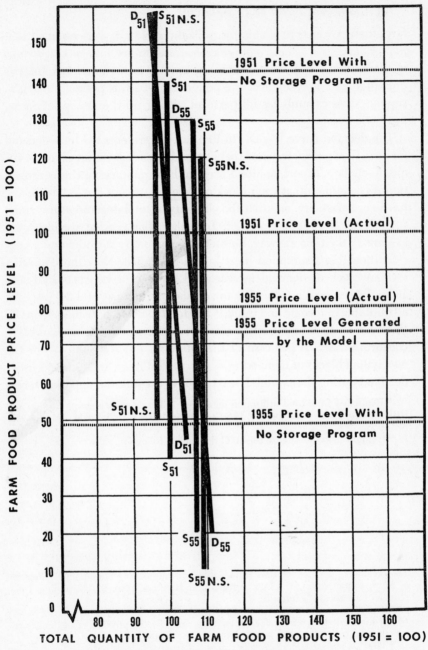

Figure 11. Farm food product price level generating model:
a working model for the period 1951–55.

farm food products available for utilization in 1951; it is assumed that imports and government storage operations do not influence the slope of the curve; it remains perfectly inelastic as in the empirical analysis presented in Figure 9. Over the period 1951–55 this perfectly inelastic supply curve expands by 7.3 per cent, taking up the new position S_{55} S_{55}.[11]

The demand curve $D_{51} D_{51}$ in Figure 11 represents the total demand for farm food products where that demand is made up of four blocks: domestic-civilian, export, nonfood uses, and the military. In this construction it is assumed that each block of demand, except domestic-civilian, has a zero elasticity, and that the elasticity of total demand at the going price level as of 1951 is —.08.[12] In reality, this is what we implicitly assume all the time anyway, but in the econometric [13] model under consideration this assumption must be made explicit. Now the domestic-civilian block of demand increased 11.1 per cent between 1951 and 1955: 7.4 per cent attributable to population increase, and 3.7 per cent attributable to income and trend.[14] *But total demand did not increase by this amount.* It did not for two reasons: (1) the domestic-civilian block constitutes only 64 per cent of the total and (2) the subtotal for the noncivilian blocks of demand (i.e., exports, military, and nonfood uses) declined during the period. If we take into account the opposing forces

[11] Estimated from total utilization data from Table 34 of *Measuring Supply and Utilization of Farm Commodities,* U.S.D.A. Agricultural Handbook No. 91, November 1955.

[12] It might help to visualize this total demand as follows:

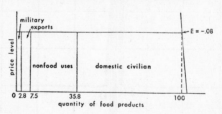

These value aggregates for 1951 from Table 34 of *Measuring Supply and Utilization of Farm Commodities,* U.S.D.A. Agricultural Handbook No. 91, November 1955, reduced to percentage form.

[13] This is a handy term used to describe the integration of three areas of work: (1) economic theory, (2) statistical analysis, and (3) the physical conditions, institutions, and technologies of some sector of the economy.

[14] The 7.4 per cent increase was computed from regularly published population data; the 3.7 per cent increase was estimated from the multiple regression equation given in Appendix Table 2 for the actual income increases and time span of the period 1951–55.

among the component blocks of demand, it turns out that total demand increased 5.2 per cent over the period 1951–55.[15] Thus, the aggregate demand relation shifts to the right, taking up the new position $D_{55} D_{55}$ in Figure 11.

The working model may now be used to generate the 1955 farm food product price level. The intersectional point of the demand relation $D_{55} D_{55}$ and the supply relation $S_{55} S_{55}$ provides the price level solution.[16] As may be observed from Figure 11, the price level generated by the model for 1955 is 73.8, indicating a decline in the farm food product price level of some 26 per cent between 1951 and 1955. This is a reasonably representative solution in terms of what actually happened between 1951 and 1955; the farm food product price level actually declined 20 per cent over this period.

Two other price level solutions of interest may be derived from the working model portrayed in Figure 11. From this model we can estimate where the farm food product price level would have gone in 1951 if we had not had a reservoir of government-held stocks to pour onto the market in that year of rapidly expanding demand, and where the farm food product price level would have gone in 1955 if the government had not removed supplies from the market and accumulated stocks in that year. The supply curve $S_{51 \text{ N.S.}} S_{51 \text{ N.S.}}$ describes the total quantity of farm food products available to satisfy total demand in 1951, under the assumption that the government stocks placed on the market that year were not in existence and therefore could not be placed on the market. The price level generated by the model in this situation is 143, indicating that the farm food product price level would have been 43 per cent higher than it was in 1951, if the government had not poured the stocks onto the market.

Similarly, the supply curve $S_{55 \text{ N.S.}} S_{55 \text{ N.S.}}$ describes the total quantity of farm food products available to satisfy total demand in 1955, assuming that the government was not accumulating stocks in price-supporting operations. In this situation, the model generates a price level of 49.3, indicating that the farm food product price level would have fallen some 50 per cent between 1951 and 1955, instead of the 20 per

---

[15] In terms of the value aggregates for 1951 given in Table 34 of U.S.D.A. Agricultural Handbook No. 91, civilian consumption increased $2436 million and non-civilian consumption decreased $670 million for a net increase of $1766 million. Hence total demand increased 5.2 per cent ($1766 ÷ $34,160 = 5.2 per cent).

[16] In this case, and all other cases, the price level solution is derived algebraically.

cent that it did, if the government had not been accumulating stocks in price-supporting operations.

Since we know that the price level solution generated by the model for 1955, for existing conditions, is some 6 per cent below the price level actually realized in 1955, it is reasonable to assume that the price level solutions presented above for the assumed no-government-stocks conditions are somewhat more extreme than the actual levels would have been, had those conditions obtained. But since the model generates a *representative* price level solution for the known situation over the period 1951–55, it seems safe to assume that the price level solutions generated for the no-government-stocks conditions are also *representative* of what would have happened if such free market conditions had prevailed.

The question may be asked at this point: Why doesn't the working model yield perfect, or near perfect, price level solutions? And the answer must be that we don't know, and can't know, given the present state of knowledge and information. We can, however, speculate on the difficulties involved. In a general sense, it is probable that the model developed here is so crude relative to the complexities of the real world, and the data used are so crude relative to the true situation, that we should not expect the model to yield perfect solutions.

But given the model presented in Figure 11, two comments may be made. It may be the case that the price elasticity of demand at the farm level is really greater than —.08; this could account for the discrepancy between the actual price level as of 1955 and the level generated by the model. Or it could be the case that the total supply relation is not perfectly inelastic; it could be that the true supply relation exhibits a slight positive slope (i.e., has a non-zero price elasticity), and that this accounts for the discrepancy. In the judgment of the author, this latter possibility seems the more plausible. On logical grounds, it seems that total supply, perhaps from increased imports if not from domestic production, should increase somewhat with a rising farm food product price level, other things being equal.

But simple as the model may be relative to the complexities of the real world, the aggregate supply and demand relations presented in Figure 11 and their movement through time, it is argued here, are *representative* of the key forces at work in the agricultural sector of the economy. The model does not replicate those forces — this a simple model cannot do. But it does represent those forces and relate them as they are related in the real world. In this sense the working model "explains" the workings of the agricultural sector of the economy at an aggregate level.

Toward a Dynamic View

More than price level solutions emerge from the working model portrayed in Figure 11 and the discussions leading up to it. Perhaps the most important consideration that emerges from that model is a way of looking at agriculture — a dynamic view. During any reasonable span of years, such as the 1951–55 period under consideration here, both aggregate demand and aggregate supply expand. Typically we find these two aggregate relations racing each other across the pages of time. Thus, except in short-run and extreme cases, the relevant question is not: How much did aggregate demand contract? and this question need never be asked with regard to aggregate supply. The relevant and important question to be asked for any typical time period is: How do the rates of expansion between aggregate demand and aggregate supply compare?

When aggregate supply is outracing demand, as it did between 1951 and 1955, then the farm price level must fall. And when aggregate demand is outracing supply, as it did between 1940 and 1945, then the farm price level must soar. Because, further, both of these aggregate relations are so extremely inelastic, any small imbalance in these rates of expansion must precipitate a wide swing in the farm level — either up or down as the imbalance dictates. The policy problem in commercial agriculture that dwarfs all others is: How may the rates of aggregate demand expansion and aggregate supply expansion be steadied and equalized at a rate that yields satisfactory prices and incomes?

4

Commodity Price Variability

An explanation for the roller-coaster-like behavior of the farm price level has now been developed and sketched. But this is only a part of the price variability problem in agriculture. Individual commodity prices bob around the moving farm price level in all manner of ways: some in an extreme fashion, some in an irregular fashion, some in a periodic fashion, and some hardly at all. So even where there is no price level problem — that is, where the price level is steady and smooth, or even better, gently upsloping — individual commodity prices vary in a variety of ways from that level. It is the task of this chapter to provide an explanation for this second form of price variability in the agricultural sector of the economy.

Since commodity prices and production are what we will be concerned with in this chapter, our unit of inquiry is conveniently defined for us. It is the individual commodity. We should recognize that we are not concerned with any, or all, aspects of commodity prices, however. We are concerned with developing an explanation for deviations of individual commodity prices from the average of all other farm commodity prices. We are concerned, therefore, with *relative prices* — how one farm commodity price varies relative to all other farm commodity prices. The analysis thus joins the main stream of economic theory at this point, for this is the kind of problem with which economic theory has traditionally been concerned: What consequences flow from a change in the price of a single commodity relative to other commodity prices? But again, as we shall see, certain peculiarities of the food and agricultural sector emerge to give the analysis of relative prices and production a special twist.

Commodities To Be Studied

Thinking back to Chapter 2, we will recall that individual commodity price variations around the moving farm price level ranged from very small to very great: whole milk prices varied as little as 6 per cent from year-to-year, and onion prices by as much as 58 per cent from year-to-year, over the long period 1920–55, with the price variability of other commodities falling into a continuum between these extremes. If time and space permitted, it might prove interesting to investigate the causes of price variability for each of the major farm commodities (it might not, too, for a great deal of repetition would be involved). But time and space do not permit, so we will investigate three commodities: potatoes, hogs, and milk. These three commodities represent respectively the different degrees of price variability found among farm commodities — extreme, moderate, and minor.

Year-to-year variations in the prices of potatoes, hogs, and whole milk, where the influence of changes in the price level have been removed, are presented in Figure 12. (Dividing the index of each commodity price by the index of prices received for all farm commodities for each year, converts the price level to a horizontal line at 100 in Figure 12, and commodity price variations to percentage deviations around it.) Some interesting facts emerge from Figure 12. Before 1940 potato prices rocket about the price level in a beautifully clear, but uncertain, cycle of two or three or four years' duration. Hog prices pursue a somewhat less extreme pattern, but a more irregular one, than do potato prices. And whole milk prices roll along like a peaceful sea.

But something happens around 1940 — war and price supports. And commodity price variability around the price level acquires a new look following 1940. During World War II, and in the years immediately after, the degree of price variability for all three commodities is reduced importantly. By 1950 the older patterns of price variability have reasserted themselves, but with potatoes on a new and relatively lower plane.

Our problem is, then, Can we find, or develop, an analysis which provides an adequate explanation of the price behavior of three such diverse commodities as potatoes, hogs and milk? Within limits the answer is yes. That analysis is to be found in part, at least, in the rigorous cobweb theorem, and in part in the degeneration of the cobweb in the real world of food and agriculture.

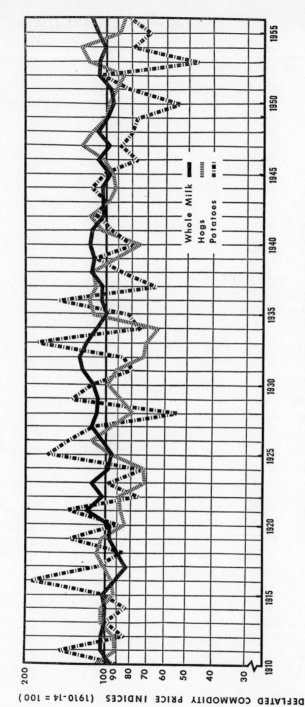

Figure 12. Commodity price indices expressed as percentages of the index of prices received for all commodities, 1910–56.

62

The Cobweb Analysis

THE CONCEPT

In the late 1930s Mordecai Ezekiel formulated the cobweb theorem to explain commodity price-output sequences in agriculture.[1] This framework of analysis has been employed by many persons since that time to unravel such sequences.[2] The cobweb analysis is an equilibrium type of analysis, making use of the traditional concepts of demand and supply. But, whereas the typical demand and supply analysis is static (e.g., the illustrative model of Figure 10, Chapter 3), the cobweb analysis is semi-dynamic; it is concerned with price-output sequences through time where the relevant demand and supply relations do not shift during the time span under consideration. This partially dynamic analysis facilitates the formulation of an explanation of price-output behavior in agriculture where a *growth period*, often a season in length but perhaps longer, separates the decisions to produce and the decisions to sell a finished product. The working of a distinct and disjointed production period, recurring periodically, into the analysis to correspond to such production periods in agriculture is, no doubt, the novel aspect of the cobweb framework of analysis.

Not so generally recognized, but central to the cobweb analysis, are two different but related concepts of supply. It takes two concepts of supply, related in a time sequence, to make the analysis go. First, we have a supply relation which describes those quantities of a commodity that farmers *plan* to produce at varying prices. It is a planning curve, to which we give the name *schedule of intentions to produce*. Second, we have a supply relation which describes at the close of the growth or production period those quantities of a commodity that farmers stand ready to offer on the market at varying prices. And since it is assumed (1) that most farm products are perishable and (2) that farmers have poor storage facilities, it is further assumed that this second supply relation, to which we give the name *market supply curve*, is severely or perfectly inelastic. Armed with these two concepts of supply, we can now take a trial spin around the cobweb.

[1] "The Cobweb Theorem," *Quarterly Journal of Economics*, February 1938, pp. 255–280.

[2] It provides, for example, the basic framework of analysis for the policy study of the potato industry under price supports by Gray, Sorenson, and Cochrane, *An Economic Analysis of the Impact of Government Programs on the Potato Industry of the United States*, Minn. Agri. Exp. Sta. Tech. Bul. 211, June 1954.

THE COBWEB ILLUSTRATED

Two cobweb models are presented in Figure 13; later we will draw certain comparisons between these models, but for the present, and for exposition purposes, let us concentrate on model I. To get under way in this analysis we must arbitrarily break into the continuing price-output sequence at some point in time, and this we do at price P_o in year 0. Price P_o in year 0 induces farmers to plan to produce quantity Q_1 in year 1. This quantity information we read off the schedule of intentions to produce curve $S_I S_I$, which describes those quantities of this commodity that farmers intend to produce at varying prices.

Now let us assume that the farmers' intentions to produce are just realized, and that quantity Q_1 is forthcoming in year 1. This quantity comes to market in a rush — is dumped onto the market — since it is assumed that the commodity is perishable and farmers lack adequate storage facilities. Thus, in fact, the market supply curve in year 1 is perfectly inelastic and is described in model I by the line $Q_1 S_m$. The market supply curve intersects the demand curve for the commodity at price P_1; this intersectional point provides the price solution for year 1. Farmers receive price P_1 for an output of Q_1 in year 1. Price P_1 in year 1 now induces farmers to plan to produce Q_2 in year 2. This quantity sells in turn at a price P_2 in year 2. The cobweb is forming, and will continue until something comes along to break it.

It will be observed that the price-output path of model II differs markedly from that of model I. Model II is convergent; model I is explosive. Now why does the price-output path of model II converge on its equilibrium position, and the price-output path of model I explode? The answer is to be found in the relative slopes of the demand relation and the schedule of intentions to produce. Whenever the slope of the schedule of intentions to produce exceeds (i.e., is steeper than) the slope of the demand relation, the price-output path converges. And, of course, whenever the slope of the demand relation exceeds that of the schedule of intentions to produce, the opposite is true. Finally, in that unlikely case where the slopes of the two curves are identical, the cobweb action goes on endlessly in the same track.

In the world of reality, it seems reasonable to assume that most commodity cobweb patterns are of the model II type. This must be the case; otherwise agriculture would be flying apart. True, price variability is extreme for certain agricultural commodities, but to date agriculture has

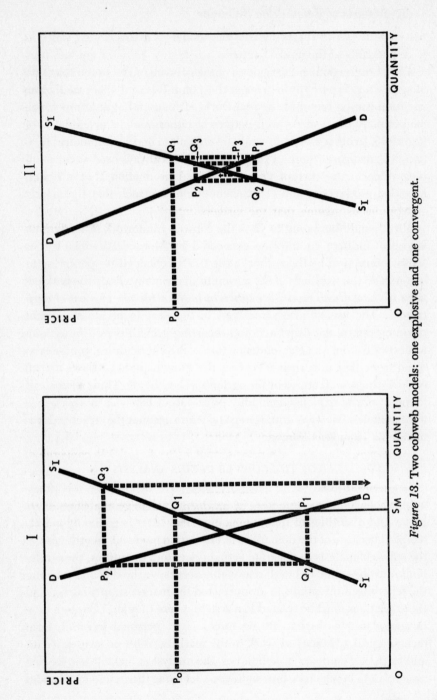

Figure 13. Two cobweb models: one explosive and one convergent.

not exploded. And this would be the tendency if commodity patterns were generally of the model I type.

A brief digression on the relation of the cobweb model to the structure of agriculture is perhaps in order at this point. It is probably true that no situation can be found in the real world of food and agriculture which fits perfectly the neat cobweb pattern of either model I or model II of Figure 13. In other words, it would be difficult to find a commodity situation in agriculture where (1) last year's price is always used as the planning price in the current year, (2) actual production always equals intended production, and (3) the conditions are such that the market supply curve is always perfectly inelastic.

But it would be wrong to view the cobweb framework of analysis as a Rube Goldberg contraption concocted by Mordecai Ezekiel in the 1930s and revived by the author in the 1950s to bedevil people trying to understand the workings of the agricultural economy. *The principal features of the cobweb model are inherent in the structure of most of agriculture.* The use of prices received in the past to arrive at current planning prices, the disjointed and recurring growth period in agricultural production, and the tendency for finished agricultural products to come to market in a rush following the growth period — these are all typical structural features of the agricultural economy. Thus, an analysis that purports to explain commodity price-output behavior in agriculture must assume a cobweb form. It must take into account the structural features built into agriculture.

USE OF THE COBWEB IN THIS ANALYSIS

The cobweb analysis is generally used to conceptualize the price-output behavior of a commodity in agriculture, not to generate the actual prices and quantities of that commodity. The latter is generally not attempted because of the difficulties of estimation involved. In order to use the cobweb analysis to generate actual prices and quantities, three relations must be estimated with reasonable accuracy: the demand relation, the schedule of intentions to produce, and the market supply curve. And these relations must be related in a system where they shift through time in accordance with the shifting forces (e.g., personal incomes, farm technological advance) at work in the markets. With present-day data and statistical estimating techniques, the analyst is lucky to derive one such relation in which he has confidence, let alone three; and his chances of replicating the system at work through time for some commodity are slim indeed. In short, with the present state of econometric knowledge, the estimating problems are simply insurmountable; this is why the cobweb is not used to predict actual price-quantity sequences.

The cobweb analysis can, however, be used to conceptualize the price-output behavior of a commodity, and such will be its use here. The cobweb analysis will be used to describe, and in this sense explain, the *degree* or *extent* of commodity price variability around the moving farm price level for potatoes, hogs, and milk. As used here, the cobweb framework is positioned astride the farm price level — the intersection of the demand curve and the schedule of intentions to produce is positioned at the price level. In this context, the price-output behavior generated by the cobweb around the price level becomes an explanation of the degree of commodity price variability around this price level. In other words, it is assumed here that the farm price level is perfectly horizontal (this is the implicit assumption of all orthodox economic theory), and the cobweb framework of analysis is used to explain the extent of relative price deviations from that price level.

Models I and II in Figure 13 cannot, however, be used to describe actual patterns of price variability through dated time. They cannot because price variability patterns result from shifts in the three relations involved as well as the price-output path around the cobweb, and in those semi-dynamic models the demand and supply relations hold fixed positions through time. We will, as a second step in these commodity analyses, however, consider the price variability patterns *and their unpredictable characteristics,* which result from the breakdown of the cobweb models through dated time.

The commodity analyses that follow thus begin with a cobweb model of the commodity. The price-output path around the model describes or explains the extent of price variability from the farm price level for the commodity. The analysis in each case then proceeds to break down the cobweb model, as the cobweb structure of the commodity in the real world might be expected to break down with the passage of time. From this second phase of the analysis we gain insights into the actual patterns of price variability for agricultural commodities.

Estimates of demand elasticity for each commodity analysis were obtained from published studies, and are cited in each instance. The schedules of intentions to produce used in each commodity analysis were estimated for this chapter, and the statistical analyses are presented in Appendix A. It is assumed that the market supply curve is perfectly inelastic in each commodity analysis; this is the conventional assumption, but in reality these market supply curves need not be, and probably are not, completely inelastic. The true elasticities of these market curves defy estimation at the present time, however.

The Cobweb Analysis for Potatoes
THE MODEL

A two-year cobweb model for potatoes is presented in Figure 14. In this model, price P_o in year 0 induces some quantity Q_1 in year 1; that quantity sells for some price P_1 in year 1; that price in turn induces some quantity Q_2 in year 2; the loop is completed in two years with price P_2. This model is consistent with the growth period in potato production; potatoes are planted, grown, and sold in one year. And it is generally hypothesized that potato prices in the previous year, or the previous two years, cause farmers to produce the quantity of potatoes that they do in the current period. In short, the model appears to fit the facts of the world reasonably well.

The potato cobweb model is positioned astride the farm price level, where that level is equal to 100. Price deviations from 100 represent relative price changes — changes in the price of potatoes relative to the average of all farm prices. The elasticity of demand at the farm level, that is at the point where price equals 100 and quantity equals 100 in Figure 14, is —.28.[3] The elasticity of the schedule of intentions to produce at the point where price equals 100 and quantity equals 100 is .25.[4] With the slope of the demand relation a bit more gentle than the schedule of intentions to produce, the potato model is convergent. Since the slopes of the two relations are nearly the same, however, and both are rather inelastic, the price-output path does converge slowly. And during the slow convergent process the price of potatoes gyrates around the price level in a wide orbit.

Beginning the price-output sequence for potatoes at a relative price of 120 is completely arbitrary. But each of the other commodity analyses

[3] Estimate by Milton Shuffett from *The Demand and Price Structure for Selected Vegetables*, U.S.D.A. Tech. Bul. 1105, and presented by Richard Foote in *Price Elasticities of Demand for Nondurable Goods with Emphasis on Food*, U.S.D.A., AMS–96, March 1956, p. 31.

[4] Refer to Appendix A for a discussion of method and relevant statistical measures.

in this chapter originates at the relative price of 120, too. A comparison of the three analyses makes clear that the price-output orbit for potatoes is wider than for the other commodities. Thus, a logical explanation emerges out of the cobweb analysis for the extreme year-to-year variations in potato prices around the farm price level. Basically the explanation grows out of the low elasticities of demand and of the schedule of intentions to produce, and the assumption of complete inelasticity for the market supply relation. This particular set of relations linked together in a dynamic, recursive system [5] provides a logical explanation for the wide relative price movements for potatoes.

BREAKING THE MODEL AND THE CONSEQUENCES

The potato model presented in Figure 14 would in time converge on the price level and thus eliminate potato price variations around the price level. It might take a long time, but, *if the model remained intact,* it would occur. Further, it might be noted that, if the slopes of the demand relation and the schedule of intentions to produce were identical, the price-output path would fall into an endless, but *regular,* two-year cycle. To such a cycle producers could adjust with certainty; the situation might be likened to that of a wage earner who *regularly* receives a large check on the first of the month and a small check in the middle of the month. He might prefer that the payments were evened out, but he could adjust to this regular but uneven flow of income.

Something, therefore, must be missing from the analysis to this point. The cobweb model of Figure 14 does not generate the pattern of price variability that we find in the real world. Except for the brief World War II period, year-to-year variations in potato prices around the farm price level have not dampened down. Furthermore, historical potato price variations do not fall into a neat, regular, two-year cycle; on the contrary, they fall into unpredictable two-, three-, or even four-year cycles.

The logical construction of Figure 14 is all right as far as it goes; it simply does not go far enough. Over a period of time the cobweb breaks down to yield an irregular pattern of price variability for a number of

[5] The idea of a recursive system is discussed in Appendix A, and it is thoroughly developed by Herman Wold and Lars Jureen in *Demand Analysis* (New York: John Wiley and Sons, 1953), Chapters 2 and 3. In general terms, however, a recursive system is one where events grow out of one another in an orderly and nonreversible progression.

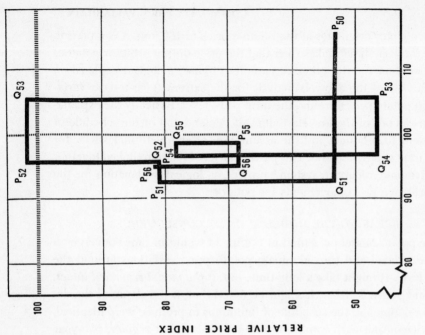

INDEX OF ACRES PLANTED

Figure 15. The actual price-output path for potatoes, 1950–56.

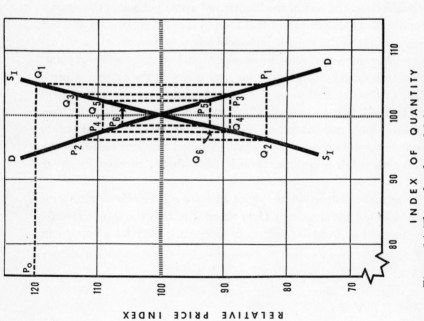

INDEX OF QUANTITY

Figure 14. The cobweb model for potatoes.

70

reasons. But three broad, generic reasons are given here. First, and probably most common, is a change in the demand for the commodity. If the demand for potatoes changes during the growing period, the regular price-output path will be broken. In Figure 14, for example, a contraction in demand during the growing season of year 1 would mean that quantity Q_1 would not sell at price P_1, but rather at some lower price.

Second, a change in the schedule of intentions to produce from one year to the next, owing perhaps to an important technological advance, breaks the neat cobweb pattern. Again in terms of Figure 14, an expansion in the schedule of intentions to produce between year 1 and year 2 would mean that price P_1 would not induce quantity Q_2, but rather would induce some output greater than Q_2.

Third, up to this point it has been implicitly assumed that the planned quantity of output would in each case be just realized. In other words, it has been assumed that the planned output Q_1 in Figure 3 would in fact be realized. But there are many reasons why this might not happen. And weather is perhaps the most important. Better or poorer than average weather may well upset production plans and give rise to a larger or smaller output than was planned. In short, realized output in any one year may deviate from planned output and break the cobweb pattern. For these general reasons, growing out of a variety of specific causes, the regular price-output path of the cobweb model may be broken. And breaking the regular price-output path brings about a jumbled, irregular pattern of price variability — how jumbled depends upon the circumstances of the breaks.

Where relative prices vary from production period to production period in a wide and unpredictable fashion, uncertainty is created in the minds of producers. Past prices become a poor guide to planning the current year's, or period's, production. The farmer becomes uncertain as to whether prices will hold up, rise, or fall in future periods. The price system ceases to be a useful and effective allocator of productive resources. Highly variable and highly uncertain commodity prices force farmers to fall back on hunches and other arbitrary guides in planning production. So it turns out that price uncertainty itself serves to break down the regular cobweb pattern, and thus produce further uncertainty.

The actual price-output path for potatoes over the period 1950–56 is presented in Figure 15. Here we have a three-year cycle followed by a two-year cycle, with both cycles falling below the farm price level as

71

suggested by the historical data of Figure 12. In the first cycle, relative prices rise from P_{50} to P_{51} to P_{52} and then fall by more than 50 per cent to P_{53}; the price rise from P_{51} to P_{52} must have resulted from an important increase in demand, since production increased in 1952 as would be expected. The price-output path converges sharply in the second cycle, and then begins to expand again in the third and unfinished cycle. Potato producers get precious little information from Figure 15 on which to base price and income expectations.

The events of the real world break down the logical construction presented in Figure 14, but these events do not lessen year-to-year potato price variations. Since the price scales in Figures 14 and 15 are the same, it can be seen that the events of the real world give rise to a wider range of relative price variability than the range suggested by the arbitrary point of origin, price 120, in the cobweb model. In the 1950s, as in the years prior to World War II, relative potato prices (i.e., actual prices deflated for changes in the price level) can change by more than 50 per cent in one year without too much trouble. This is real price variability.

The Cobweb Analysis for Hogs
THE MODEL

A two-year cobweb model for hogs is presented in Figure 16. The price-output sequence of this model does not, however, represent full year units of time. The cycle in Figure 16 relates to the spring pig crop, which goes to market during the period August through January. Thus, the price P_o is for the period August through January of year 0; this price induces farmers to produce a spring pig crop Q_1 which goes to market during the period August through January of year 1; and so on around the cobweb. This model is probably not absolutely consistent with the time periods involved in producing and marketing the spring pig crop; the prices that influence farmers to breed sows for the spring pig crop may precede the August–January period somewhat, and marketings from the spring pig crop may lap over the end of that six-month period somewhat. But granted some latitude in the facts of the situation, this model fits the time schedule of gestation, animal growth, and marketing peaks reasonably well.

As in the case of potatoes, the cobweb model for the spring pig crop is positioned astride the farm price level where that level is equal to

100. Price deviations from 100 represent relative price changes — changes in the price of fall marketed hogs relative to the average of all farm prices. The elasticity of demand at the farm level, that is at the point where price equals 100 and quantity equals 100, in Figure 16, is —.55.[6] The elasticity of the schedule of intentions to produce a spring pig crop at the point where price equals 100 and quantity equals 100, is .31.[7] With the slope of the demand relation significantly less steeply inclined than the schedule of intentions to produce in this model, the price-output path is strongly convergent.

There is still room for some price variability around the farm price level in this model, but compared with the potato model in Figure 14, it generates a restricted orbit of price variability. This is consistent with the comparative data on relative price variability. It will be recalled from Chapter 2 that the average year-to-year percentage variation in potato prices around the moving farm price level is 49 per cent for the period 1920 to 1955, whereas the average variation is only 15 per cent for hogs for the same period. In sum, the relative elasticities of demand and the schedule of intentions to produce employed in the hog cobweb model ensure some price variability around the farm price level, but considerably less than for potatoes.

BREAKING THE MODEL AND THE CONSEQUENCES

Again the model presented in Figure 16 does not provide an adequate explanation of commodity price variability. Left alone, the price-output path of the cobweb model would converge on the price level, eliminating all further variability. Further, and more important, price variability for hogs does not fall into a regular two-year pattern; a glance at Figure 12 makes this clear. Hog price variability around the farm price level moves through unpredictable patterns of four, five, six, or even seven years' duration.

But this can be explained again in terms of a breakdown of the cobweb model. It is unreasonable to assume that the demand relation and the schedule of intentions to produce in Figure 16 would hold fixed positions over four or five years, thus permitting the price-output path to converge on the farm price level. In the real world of food and agriculture, the demand relation probably shifts every year, and the schedule

[6] Estimate by Elmer Learn, "Estimating Demand of Livestock Products," *Journal of Farm Economics*, Proceedings Issue, December 1956, p. 1488.

[7] See Appendix A for a discussion of method and relevant statistical measures.

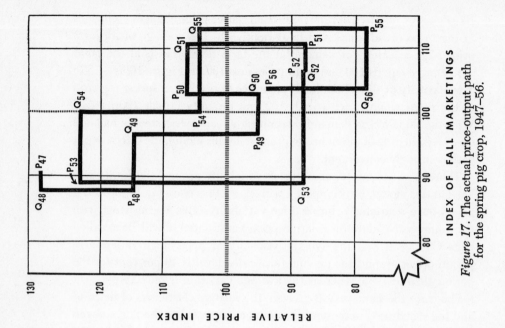

Figure 17. The actual price-output path for the spring pig crop, 1947–56.

INDEX OF FALL MARKETINGS

RELATIVE PRICE INDEX

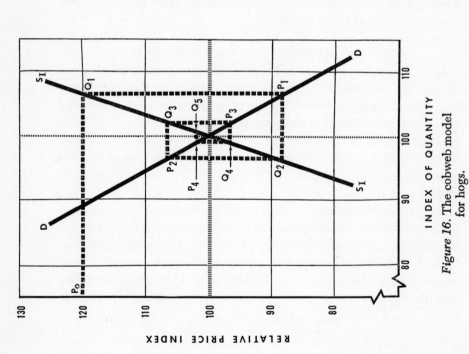

Figure 16. The cobweb model for hogs.

INDEX OF QUANTITY

RELATIVE PRICE INDEX

74

of intentions to produce shifts with changes in the price of the principal hog input — corn. The schedule of intentions to produce will expand with a fall in the price of corn, indicating a willingness on the part of farmers to produce more hogs at any given price of hogs, and conversely. And corn prices, resulting from cycles in the weather, often move in the same direction for two or more years. Consequently, such shifts in these relations break down the predictable two-year pattern of price variability and replace it with an unpredictable pattern of four, five, six, or even seven years' duration.

It is also probably the case that the market supply curve is not perfectly inelastic in the case of hogs. In fact, it may exhibit a negative slope at times: in periods of high or rising prices, farmers tend to hold back gilts and sows from the market for breeding purposes, while in periods of low prices they ship off their breeding stock. For this reason, too, the regular cobweb interaction portrayed in Figure 16 is riddled and replaced by an irregular pattern.

The forces represented by the demand relation, the schedule of intentions to produce, and the market supply curve in the hog cobweb model are all at work in the hog-corn sector, and they are related in the recursive form implied by the cobweb theorem; but the price-output path of the model is not replicated in the market. It cannot be; with the passage of time numerous events that break down the model can and do occur in the market.

The actual price-output path for the spring pig crop over the period 1947–56 is presented in Figure 17. This path describes the relative price for hogs during the period August 1947–January 1948 (P_{47} in Figure 17) which induces farmers to produce and sell the quantity marketed during the period August 1948–January 1949 (Q_{48} in Figure 17), and so on along the realized path.

Several points may be made with respect to the actual price-output path for spring pigs. First, it bears no resemblance to the clear cobweb pattern of Figure 16; it winds around in an apparently irrational fashion. Second, it does not converge as does the cobweb model. Third, the relative price of hogs may be expected to change 10 to 20 per cent each year, and in either direction, but the pattern of variability is considerably less for hogs than for potatoes (compare Figures 15 and 17). In sum, the relative price variability for hogs is not so great as for potatoes, but in some ways it is more unpredictable.

75

The Cobweb Analysis for Milk

Milk fits the cobweb framework of analysis least well of the three commodities under consideration. The cobweb analysis assumes a definite growth period in the production process interspersed between the decisions to produce and the decisions to sell, recurring in a periodic fashion; the juxtaposition of these events is what creates the cobweb. But milk production does not occur in distinct and disjointed time periods; it flows endlessly on. Certainly there is seasonality in milk production, but this complicates rather than eases the problem of fitting milk into the cobweb analysis, for seasonality in milk production grows out of the seasons, not out of economic decision-making.

The major question to be answered in constructing a cobweb analysis for milk is what time period to use. If the analyst is thinking in terms of variations in output growing out of variations in numbers of cows, or some sort of a dairy cattle cycle, then the time span must be very long. And the schedule of intentions to produce must be estimated so as to permit cattle numbers to vary. But past efforts in this direction have been fruitless and frustrating.[8] On the other hand, if the analyst is thinking in terms of variations in output (i.e., seasonally adjusted output) growing out of variations in feeding rates, then the time span must be very short — perhaps a month; the assumption here being that the last milk check influences feeding rates. The cobweb analysis developed in this chapter for milk is something of a compromise between these views, but leans toward the latter.

The cobweb model for milk presented in Figure 18 involves a six-month cycle: two periods, each three months in duration. All prices and outputs are seasonally adjusted to remove that complicating and noneconomic factor from the analysis. Price P_0 in the last quarter of year 0, it is assumed, induces farmers to try to produce quantity Q_1 in the first quarter of year 1; quantity Q_1 sells for a price P_1 in the first quarter; this price P_1 induces farmers to try to produce quantity Q_2 in the second quarter, and so on around the cobweb.

There are problems with this model; it is not consistent with some disjointed and periodic production period, since none exists. But it is not useless. In the first place, milk prices in one three-month period must influence output in the next period through feeding rates and culling

---

[8] Estimates of milk supply relations where numbers of cows are not held constant are as likely to have a negative sign as a positive one.

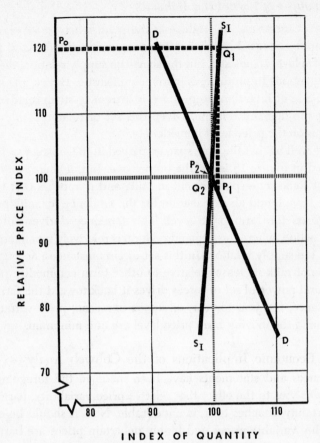

Figure 18. The cobweb model for milk.

rates, if price has any effect on milk production. Second, the idea of a perfectly inelastic market-supply relation makes good sense for a highly perishable commodity like milk. Third, the estimates of the demand relation and the schedule of intentions to produce employed in this model appear, on the basis of past experience, to be reasonable.

As in previous commodity analyses, the milk cobweb model is positioned astride the farm price level where that level is equal to 100. Price deviations from 100 represent relative price changes — changes in the price of milk relative to the average of all farm prices. The elasticity of demand at the farm level, that is at the point where price equals 100 and quantity equals 100, in Figure 18, is —.38.[9] The elasticity of the

[9] Learn, *op. cit.*, p. 1488.

schedule of intentions to produce at the point where price equals 100 and quantity equals 100 is .03.[10] In other words, the demand relation at the farm level is inelastic, but the short-run supply relation, the schedule of intentions to produce, is extremely inelastic. Hence, the slope of the schedule of intentions to produce is extremely steep relative to the slope of the demand relation. Given this set of relations, the cobweb converges on the price level immediately.

It may well be that the time span employed in the milk cobweb model portrayed in Figure 18 is not the proper one. But, if there is a cobweb action of some time span present in milk, and it appears that there is, then we have found an explanation for the tendency for milk prices to converge on the farm price level. This tendency derives out of the cobweb action, where the demand relation is relatively much more elastic than the supply relation. In this set of circumstances, any time that the price of milk increases relative to other farm commodity prices, a unique and powerful set of forces drives it back toward the farm price level. Hence, the year-to-year, or season-to-season, price variations of milk around the moving farm price level are at a minimum.

Economic Implications of the Cobweb Analyses

Inferences and statements have been made in the foregoing commodity analyses to the effect that relative price variability, particularly as uncertainty attaches to it, is undesirable. Now it should be obvious that highly variable prices and highly uncertain prices are harmful to producers. But all relative price changes — that is, changes in one commodity price relative to all others — are not bad. On the contrary, relative price changes are an essential part of economic change and development. Relative price changes guide and direct resources into those productive uses that maximize the total utility of society; relative price changes effect, or induce, wanted changes in the composition of total output.

A relative price increase growing out of an increase in demand resulting in turn from increased consumer preference, which induces farmers to shift resources into the production of that commodity and increase its output, means that the pricing system is properly performing one of the important roles assigned to it by society in a mixed-enterprise, capitalistic economy like ours. Or a relative price decrease growing out of

[10] See Appendix A for a discussion of method and relevant statistical measures.

an increase in supply resulting in turn from a technological advance, which induces farmers to shift some resources out of the production of this commodity and decrease its output, means also that the pricing system is functioning properly. In these examples, relative price changes are facilitating or inducing changes in resource combinations in accordance with the dictates of a changing world. This is what we want from the pricing system.

Thus we should not, and cannot, subscribe to the view that all price changes are undesirable. Relative price changes are indispensable to economic change and development.

But incessant commodity price gyrations around the farm price level, extreme and unpredictable in nature, are undesirable. Extreme and irregular relative price changes create uncertainty — undue uncertainty — in the minds of producers, and this leads to two kinds of inefficiency. First, the producer is handicapped with respect to planning next year's production. Last year's prices are of little or no use to him. He must guess at some most probable set of prices for planning purposes — probably a discounted set of last year's prices — and this set of prices may not reflect the wants of society.

Second, uncertainty in the minds of farm producers leads to an unwillingness on their part to invest in costly new production techniques, or to assume long-term financial commitments associated with new and improved production techniques. Farm businessmen like other businessmen hesitate to invest heavily in risky enterprises; hence the adoption of improved production techniques is often delayed. Price and income risks arising out of price uncertainty have the effect of slowing down technological advance in farming.

Price and income risk arising out of price uncertainty may be viewed as a social cost, but it is a cost that must be borne entirely by the producers of the commodities involved. Such costs have two effects: (1) they distort the allocation of resources and (2) they slow down technological advance. The cost of risk in commodities with highly variable and highly uncertain prices has the effect first of reducing the employment of inputs in that commodity relative to other less risky commodities, and second, increasing the cost of, or reducing the flow of, new capital investments into the enterprise. Thus, we conclude that extreme and irregular relative price changes arising out of a broken cobweb interaction leads to widespread inefficiencies.

It is difficult to say how important these risk-induced inefficiencies may be. There can be no doubt that they are widespread. Several million farmers in many commodity lines are involved. But what these inefficiencies add up to in the way of reduced real incomes and reduced human satisfaction is impossible to say. Perhaps about all that can be said is that price and income uncertainty results in some annoyance to a great number of farmers, a great deal of annoyance to some farmers, and almost no annoyance to nonfarm people.

The Commodity Parts of the Aggregative Analysis

The relationship of the individual commodity analyses to the aggregative analysis will now be developed. In a way, this has already been done, since the commodity analyses of this chapter describe output changes in response to relative price changes — changes in the price of one commodity relative to all others (i.e., the aggregate). But it may help to construct, so to speak, the aggregative analysis out of the individual commodity parts. In other words, the logical consistency of the general theory of farm prices may be enhanced by a thorough understanding of the relationship of the parts to the whole.

THE CONSTRUCTION PROCESS

The supply relation — the schedule of intentions to produce which describes the intentions of farmers to produce a commodity as its price varies relative to the prices of other commodities — generally exhibits some positive price elasticity. In other words, farmers *plan* to produce more of a commodity when the price of it increases relative to the prices of commodity substitutes, and conversely. And these plans are realized on multiple enterprise units by farmers shifting resources among enterprises, and in agriculture generally by farmers lending, renting, and selling resources among themselves. But the market supply curve, which describes the flow of products to market at the end of the production period, is highly inelastic. The extreme inelasticity of the market supply curve results from the perishable nature of most farm products, and their rush to market at the end of the growing period.

Now let us assume a rapid and important increase in the demand for all food, resulting, say, from a decision on the part of the United States to feed a large part of the world, which is precisely what happened during and following World War II. In such a situation the demand for each food item probably would not increase proportionately, but each would increase and that is the important point for this discussion. Given a sharp and general increase in the demand for food in one year, the relatively elastic schedules of intentions to produce do not describe the output responses to this increase in demand. They cannot, because decisions to produce will have already been translated into actions to produce, and production processes will have been set in motion for the year.

In the short run of the year, the market supply curves describe, commodity by commodity, the nature of the supply response. And they are highly, or perfectly, inelastic. Thus, demand relations, commodity by commodity, will, in this assumed situation, ride up highly inelastic supply relations and drive prices up, commodity by commodity. The result is a higher farm price level and little or no increase in aggregate output. This result is consistent with some things we already know: (1) that the aggregate supply relation for farm products is highly, or perfectly, inelastic in the short run; and (2) that during wide sweeps in the farm price level, individual commodity prices pull together and move in a parallel fashion.

But this intra-year analysis does not go to the heart of the problem. Assuming that this general expansion in the demand for food extends over several years and, to keep our thinking straight, assuming also that there is no technological advance, then the relatively elastic schedules of intentions to produce again fail to describe the output responses of individual commodities to the general increase in demand. The schedules of intentions to produce cannot describe the planned output responses in this situation, *because each describes the planned output response of a commodity on the assumption that only the price of that one commodity is changing (i.e., that we have a relative price change).* But in this assumed situation all farm prices are rising. True, all farm prices may not be rising at the same rate; hence there may be some shifting of resources among enterprises with some change in the composition of total output. But equally true, the output of each enterprise on each farm cannot expand, as described by the relevant schedule of intentions to produce, as all commodity prices rise, unless the total complex of resources used in agricultural production is increased during the period. And the latter is clearly impossible.

Thus, in the short run of several years, the market supply curves once again take over and describe supply behavior, commodity by commodity. And demand relations, commodity by commodity, ride up these highly inelastic market supply relations and drive prices up, commodity by commodity. The consequences of a general increase in the demand for food over several years is thus the same as for one year: a higher farm price level and little or no increase in aggregate output. And this result, too, is consistent with some things we already know: (1) the aggregate supply relation for farm products may hold a fixed and highly inelastic position over several years, and (2) total resources employed in agriculture typically do not expand during good times in agriculture — typically total resource inputs in agriculture hold constant.

Now let us assume another, and very different, situation. Let us assume that the total demand for farm food products is constant, unchanging. And similarly that total supply is unchanging. In other words, changes in the farm price level are assumed away, by assuming away changes in over-all demand resulting from changes in national income or population, and by assuming away changes in over-all supply resulting from changes in total resources employed or in technological advance. But changes within the aggregate may be expected to occur: the demand for a particular commodity may expand or contract because of a change in consumer preferences for it; a crop failure in one commodity may occur alongside a bumper crop in another commodity; or disease control may greatly increase the cost of production of some commodity. Any one of the above causal events could set off a cobweb action for the commodity involved, leading to a relative price change, resource shifts among enterprises, changes in the output of the commodity, then relative price change again, and so on. In other words, in this context the schedule of intentions to produce does describe the planned output responses of farmers, and the schedule of intentions to produce in conjunction with the demand relation for the commodity sets up a cobweb interaction leading to *shifts in the composition of total output and variations in commodity prices around the price level.*

In connection with these two assumed cases, it might prove interesting to refer back to Figure 2 of Chapter 2 (p. 14) and once again observe the tendency for the various farm commodity prices to pull together and move together in times of major movements in the farm price level, and to gyrate around the farm price level during periods of price level stability.

THE SEA OF COMPETITIVE BEHAVIOR

The commodity parts of agriculture flow together into a sea of competitive behavior. The ubiquitous process of substitution — the substitution of cheap for dear food items on the demand side, and the substitution of more profitable for less profitable enterprises on the supply side — works impersonally and endlessly to stabilize commodity prices at sea level within the agricultural aggregate. Whitecaps and troughs dot this sea, which from time to time becomes a little rough; all of this, however, may be explained by the workings of the various commodity cobwebs. But powerful forces — competitive forces involving substitution — are forever leveling the whitecaps and filling in the troughs.

With these competitive forces at work in a great sea like American agriculture, studying one commodity is like studying one whitecap in the Pacific Ocean; it merges into the larger sea in an infinite number of ways, leaving the analyst with nothing to study. The sense of futility which overtakes the analyst and student alike in studying the market behavior of individual commodities in agriculture is evident in this chapter. One can trace the consequences of some event to a commodity through dated time for a brief period, but soon the consequences of this event in the market are lost in the maze of other consequences resulting from numberless other events, all tied together or integrated into a meaningful whole by an infinity of resource and product substitutions. Unraveling the market behavior — the price-output behavior — of a commodity in this seamless web is hopeless.

Within the agricultural sea of competitive behavior the economy operates, with the exception of the cobweb interaction, just about as the classical and neo-classical economists said it does and implied that it *should*. This agricultural sea that we have been talking about differs, however, from the seas that ships sail on and the sea of competitive behavior that the classicals implicitly assumed. The level of the agriculture sea rises and falls, and sometimes sharply, and it can remain low relative to other seas — that is, other sectors of the economy — for extended periods. The price level of this agricultural sea, to push this analogy just a little further, is a stormy one. When it rises it brings prosperity to all farmers, efficient and inefficient alike, and when it falls it brings despair to all farmers and failure to many. Changes in the level of farm prices create income problems ignored and/or assumed away by the classical and neo-classical economists.

An Analysis of Farm Price Behavior

Now changes in the level of farm prices, where they all act together, can be analyzed and explained in terms of the behavior of each individual commodity, as was done in the previous section. But this is a cumbersome procedure. It is easier, much easier, to treat all food as one big commodity, and to relate the demand for all food to the supply of all food. (Here we assume that the aggregate food is synonymous with agriculture; this, of course, is not entirely true, but the tobacco and fiber exceptions do not impair the logic of the argument.)

And there are logical grounds for treating all food as one big commodity. The high degree of product and enterprise substitutability which exists within agriculture, and fuses the commodity parts into a sea of competitive behavior, does not extend across the agricultural sector to other sectors of the economy. Resources transfer across the farm-nonfarm line, but not nearly so easily as among enterprises within agriculture. And the substitution of food items for nonfood items, and conversely, is certainly at a minimum. So it is appropriate to visualize the food and agricultural sector as a self-contained sea, where the substitutional possibilities within the sector are varied and numberless, but the substitutional possibilities across the sector line are limited and restrained.

This was the view taken in the aggregative analysis of Chapter 3. The aggregate demand for the big commodity food was related to the aggregate supply of the big commodity food to explain changes in the food product price level (i.e., the farm price level). And this shall be our general procedure once again in Chapter 5.

5

The Agricultural Treadmill

In this chapter we shall consider the economic position of commercial farmers in the changing, developing world. The analysis will be concerned with such things as economic growth, market organization and the process of technological advance, and the consequences of these developments for farm people. The analysis once again is aggregative in order to avoid becoming lost in the sea of competitive behavior that comprises American agriculture. But it does not again assume the form of a static supply and demand model; rather it builds on the static model in an effort to become dynamic.

The Long-Run Race between Aggregate Demand and Aggregate Supply

As we already know, the farm price level fluctuates in response to a shift in aggregate demand relative to supply, or a shift in aggregate supply relative to demand. But it is not correct to visualize these aggregate relations shifting back and forth in a static, no-growth context. Over the long run, both of these aggregate relations have been expanding: what we have had is a race between aggregate demand and aggregate supply. And changes in the farm price level that have occurred, growing out of shifts in the *relative* positions of the aggregate demand and supply relations, have most often resulted from unequal rates of expansion in these aggregate relations. The race has rarely been equal, and at times it has been very unequal, with extreme income consequences.[1]

[1] For a good discussion of the unequal rates of growth between aggregate demand and aggregate supply, see T. W. Schultz, *Agriculture in an Unstable Economy* (New York: McGraw-Hill, 1945), Chapter III.

DEMAND SHIFTERS

During the nineteenth and early twentieth centuries both rising real incomes and population growth operated to expand the aggregate demand for food. Rising real incomes enabled the average consumer to move away from a plain diet heavily weighted with potatoes and cereals to a varied and expensive diet — varied in terms of more animal products, more fruits and vegetables in and out of season, and more delicacies (cheeses, sea food, baked goods); and expensive in terms of greater dollar cost and more farm resources required to produce it. And population growth contributed more mouths to feed.

It is generally believed that the population elasticity for food approximates 1.0 — meaning that a 1 per cent increase in population growth results in a 1 per cent increase in food consumption. This population elasticity estimate will vary as the means of population growth (i.e., immigration and natural increase) varies; but it is probably a useful rule of thumb. And since the total population of the United States increased by about 2000 per cent between 1800 and 1920, it follows that the aggregate demand for food increased by roughly the same amount as the result of population growth. During this long period, the market for farm food products widened, first, because there were many more mouths to feed and, second, because each mouth demanded a more varied and expensive diet.

Now let us take a more careful look at the shifters of demand that have been at work in the first half of the twentieth century. And let us look first at the demand shifter, change in income. Sometime in our national history, the income elasticity for food fell, and fell drastically — a development that probably occurred during the decades preceding and following 1900. In other words, it is posited here that real income increases for the average consumer were so great during this period (about 100 per cent between 1880 and 1920) that the average consumer broke through, to an important degree, that income range where rising incomes shoot into the purchases of more food and more expensive food, and moved into that income range where changes in income have little effect on total food consumption. In any event, the income elasticity for *farm food products* is now in the neighborhood of 0.2 — meaning that the consumption of farm food products by the average consumer increases 2 per cent with a 10 per cent increase in his income. Consumers in the 1950s prefer to use additional income to purchase automobiles,

86

durable goods, sporting goods, vacations, and services with their food, rather than more food.

In this instance we are *not* talking about the income elasticity of food items purchased by consumers in retail stores; the income elasticity of food items purchased by consumers at retail runs about 0.6 to 0.7, and it is this high because the income elasticity for nonfarm food services associated with, or built into, those food items (i.e., storing, transporting, packaging, processing, and merchandising) is much higher — running between 1.0 and 1.3. In less technical language, consumers are ready and eager to buy more conveniences and gadgets (e.g., TV dinners) with farm food products, as their incomes rise. But they are not so willing — in fact they are reluctant — to buy more farm food products as their incomes rise.

The income elasticity of farm food products is not likely to approach zero in the late 1950s or early 1960s, but it may approach zero by 1975, and if not by 1975 then certainly by the year 2000. The income elasticity for farm food products cannot fall immediately because there were some 60 million consumers in the United States in 1955, living in families and as single individuals, with incomes of less than $3500. These are the consumers that currently increase their consumption of animal products and fresh fruits and vegetables importantly as their incomes rise. This is the group that has pulled the income elasticity for farm food products for the average consumer up to as high as 0.2 in the 1950s.

But if per capita real incomes increase by as much from 1955 to 1975 as they did from 1935 to 1955, the poorest family in 1975 will, relatively speaking, be living in grand style in that not too distant year. That is, barring a major economic depression, we can look forward to a time, perhaps by 1975 and certainly by 2000, when the basic wants of all families in the United States will have been satisfied with respect to farm food products — when the income elasticity of those products will have fallen to zero. This is not to say that the income elasticity for *nonfarm* food services will have fallen to zero. On the contrary, this latter elasticity may remain above 1.0 as more and more wives escape from the kitchen and experience the joys of dining out.

The key point to keep in mind in all this is that consumers purchase two very different categories of resources in what is commonly called food: (1) farm resources embodied in farm food products and (2) nonfarm resources converted into services associated with and built into farm food products. The consumption of the second category of resources increases at least proportionately with increases in income, but the consumption of the first category of resources increases only modestly with increases in income, and may in the foreseeable future cease to increase at all.

One qualification needs to be added to the above conclusion, and it is not a happy one. Should the economy of the United States run into a prolonged depression, the income elasticity estimate of 0.2 indicates the contractions in the purchases of farm food products that would occur with declining incomes, *until personal incomes began to fall seriously.* But once real personal incomes declined to levels substantially below those of the 1950s, the income elasticity for farm food products might be expected to rise; and a higher income elasticity would, of course, accelerate the contraction in the aggregate demand for food. So it turns out that rising real incomes now do little to expand the demand for farm food products, and may in the future do nothing; but falling real incomes under depressed economic conditions could serve to contract the aggregate demand for food, and contract it importantly.

Now we turn to the second demand shifter, population growth. Fortunately for the agricultural sector, developments with respect to population growth as a demand shifter have not paralleled those of rising real incomes. For a while it was feared that population growth as a shifter of demand was losing its power too; in the 1930s most predictions of population growth had the population of the United States leveling off and declining in the 1960s. But for some totally unexplainable reason, the people of the United States decided during and following World War II to wreck the prewar population projections of demographers by going on a child-producing spree. The rate of population increase in the United States in the 1950s is among the highest of the nations of the world — 15 per thousand as compared with 4.5 for the United Kingdom, 13 for India, and 20 for China.

In comparative terms, perhaps more relevant for this discussion, the total population of the United States increased nearly 9 per cent in the decade ending in 1935, 9 per cent in the decade ending in 1945, and 16 per cent in the decade ending 1955. And if the 1954–55 rate of increase is maintained, total population in the United States will increase by some 16 per cent in the decade ending in 1965, to reach a figure of 193 million; and by 37 per cent in the two decades from 1956 to 1975 to reach a figure of 228 million. Even if the 1954–55 rate of population increase moderates slightly, as many experts believe it will, there are still going to be many more people around in 1975 to be fed — certainly no fewer than 210 million.

The picture that emerges with respect to further expansions in the demand for food looks like this: The United States is approaching that state of opulence where further increases in real personal incomes will not act to expand the demand for food. Expansions in the aggregate demand for food are becoming dependent upon population growth alone. But during the period 1955–75, population growth is going to be a powerful force acting to increase the demand for farm food products.

One more idea should be incorporated into this discussion of the aggregate demand for food. As this aggregate demand relation expands through time, driven by population growth, it will, in all probability, become even more inelastic than it is now. Further decreases in the price elasticity of the aggregate demand for food will result from further increases in real personal incomes. As argued in Chapter 3, rising real incomes historically have had the effect of reducing the price elasticity of the aggregate demand for food, and there is every reason to believe that this tendency will continue until food, like safety pins now, has a zero price elasticity. When this happens — and the time is not too far off — if the fantastic rate of economic development of the 1946–56 period is maintained, the aggregate demand for food will expand in a perfectly inelastic manner, powered by population growth alone.

SUPPLY SHIFTERS

During the nineteenth century, total farm output in the United States increased as the result of two basic forces: (1) farm technological advance and (2) an increase in the size of the total fixed plant — an increase in the number of acres incorporated into going farm firms. The former was a minor cause and the latter the major cause. Regardless of the level of farm prices, or the pattern of commodity prices, settlers pushed back the frontier year after year and added land and farmsteads to the total fixed plant. Land settlement was part of the great westering movement in America over three centuries, and although it may have grown out of certain economic dislocation and adjustments in the Old World, it was in no way related to the pricing system, except insofar as hard times in the cities forced more people on to the frontier.

An Analysis of Farm Price Behavior

With the turn of the century, this means of expanding total farm output began to disappear — the country was almost settled. And by 1920, except for some irrigation developments in the arid West, the total agricultural plant stopped growing. Total farm output did not, however. As already noted, total farm output increased some 90 per cent between 1914 and 1956. This great increase resulted almost exclusively from technological advance on existing farms — a process that gained momentum in the latter part of the nineteenth century, in the form of farm mechanization particularly, and became an all-inclusive, ever-present force by the end of World War I. The minor force behind output expansion in the 1800s became the major force in the 1900s.

The development and adoption of many new technologies have contributed to the expansion of the total marketable output of farm commodities since 1920, but none has been so important as the tractor. The substitution of tractor power for animal power has released some 70 million acres, or one fifth of our crop land, for the production of marketable crops. And the myriad of hookups that have been developed to go with the tractor have released several million workers for nonfarm employment (a development that is sometimes considered a mixed blessing). Certainly the gasoline engine in its many forms and uses dominated farm technological advance between 1920 and 1950.

Now there are some who say, because they see evolving no single technology comparable in importance with the tractor, that farm technological advance is losing its steam, too, as a shifter of the aggregate supply relation. But people who take this view don't appreciate the extent to which the development and application of new technologies now blankets and permeates the agricultural scene. True, no single developing technology dominates the scene in the 1950s to the extent that the tractor did in the previous three decades. But one dominant technology is not a requirement of rapid technological advance, and hence of a rapid rate of output expansion. Total farm output is expanding rapidly in the 1950s as the result of technological development and adoption on many fronts: plant and animal breeding; plant and animal disease control; feeds and feeding practices; water control and usage; and soil, crop, and animal handling equipment. Advances on all of these technological fronts contribute to a situation in which the typical farmer adopts one to several new practices each year, becoming thereby a more productive farmer.

90

In this connection we should recognize, too, that the development of new technologies and their adoption on farms is no longer left to chance. The outpouring of new production practices and techniques that occurred between 1920 and 1955 did not result from the work of a few lonesome inventors in an attic or an old barn; rather it resulted from organized and well-financed research at several levels: pure research on natural phenomena, applied research on agricultural problems, and commercial research on specific products and techniques.

Private and public agencies currently spend up to $200 million, and perhaps more, each year on the development of new technologies for *farm production*.[2] And all the efforts directed toward carrying these new technologies to farmers must run into sums much larger than the $200 million. Consider all the agencies, private and public, involved: the federal-state extension service; the vocational agricultural teaching program in high schools; the soil conservation service; the service work of farm cooperatives; and, finally and probably now most important, the selling and service work of private feed firms, machinery and equipment firms, processing firms, and producer associations.

The adoption of new production techniques has become as much a part of farming as getting up in the morning; the farmer is "expected" to adopt new practices and technologies which reduce his costs and expand his output in the same way that he is "expected" to care for his livestock, send his children to school, and honor his wife; the farmer is the last link in an endless chain of events, called technological advance, which almost everyone considers good.

Those folks looking for (or trying to hide from) a second revolutionary development to follow the tractor may find it before the turn of the next century. If and when artificial photosynthesis breaks out of the laboratory, where it is now an established fact, that institution-shaking technology will have arrived. When we can produce carbohydrates directly from the sun's rays, without the work of plants, then the production of foodstuffs can be transferred from farms to factories and the greatest of all agricultural revolutions will rage across the land. And the process of artificial photosynthesis is certainly farther advanced in the 1950s than was the unleashing of the atom in 1900.

So we conclude that farm technological advance, development and

---

[2] This amount does not include funds used to finance research on the handling, processing, and distribution of products after they leave the farm.

farm adoption, gives every evidence of remaining a powerful force in agriculture, driving the aggregate supply relation before it in an expanding action. And truly revolutionary developments which could turn present-day agriculture upside down are in the offing.

THE RACE, 1955 TO 1975

The long-run race between aggregate demand and aggregate supply, thus, for all practical purposes, turns out to be a race between population growth and farm technological advance. Since, however, nobody is omniscient, it is impossible to demonstrate that population growth will outrun technological advance between 1955 and 1975, or the converse. If an observer is more impressed with the capacity of Americans to reproduce themselves than with their ability to create new ways of producing goods and services, then he will probably conclude that population growth will win the race. But if, on the other hand, he is more impressed with their inventive genius and ability to adopt new technologies, then he will probably put his money on technological advance.

Which wins is terribly important to American farmers. If population growth outraces technological advance, other things being equal, aggregate demand will press against supply and push the level of farm prices upward, as did occur between 1895 and 1915. But if technological advance outraces population growth, other things being equal, aggregate supply will press against demand and drive farm prices downward, as has been the tendency since 1948.

Some evidence can, however, be adduced about the outcome of the race between aggregate demand and aggregate supply over the period 1955–75, where conclusive proof is impossible. During the period 1951–56 total population in the United States increased by exactly 9 per cent. At the same time the total output of marketable farm products increased by 13 per cent. The figures in this comparison change somewhat depending upon the exact years chosen and the output index used, but the general picture does not change. The total output of farm products in the first half of the 1950s is outracing population growth. And this increase in total farm output occurs in the face of a declining farm price level, and with no significant increase in the total inputs employed. In the 1950s output expansion is winning the race.

James T. Bonnen, looking forward to 1965 in a major study which assesses the output expanding potential of all "known and almost known technology," suggests that the trends of the early 1950s will not be reversed.[3] Assuming that the farm price level is maintained at the 1955 level, which relatively speaking is low, Bonnen estimates that total agricultural production will increase by 30 per cent between 1955 and 1965. Taking into account an estimated 15 per cent increase in population over the period, and a 4 per cent increase in per capita food consumption, the Bonnen model indicates that the annual rate of farm surplus, which stood at 8 per cent of total supply in 1955, would be enlarged to 12 per cent as of 1965. In other words, this study, taking a comprehensive look to 1965, concludes that output expansion will increase its lead over demand expansion in the years ahead. In terms of the 1955 farm price level, the total farm surplus will increase from 8 per cent in 1955 to 12 per cent in 1965.

It is the judgment of this writer that the rate of aggregate output expansion can easily exceed the rate of aggregate demand expansion over the period 1955–75. And what can easily occur will probably occur. In this probable event, one of two things must happen: (1) the annual accumulation of surplus stocks by government must increase, or (2) the farm price level must fall. In other words, this writer believes that the expanding supply relation will press against the expanding demand relation in the long-run race between the two and either drive farm prices lower, or, at a supported price level, drive more stocks into the hands of government. The capacity to expand farm output beyond the needs of the population is there, and, unless counteracted in some effective way, this capacity will further intensify the general income problem in agriculture.

All that has been said to this point with regard to the race between the aggregate demand for and the aggregate supply of food over the period 1955–75 has assumed an expanding total economy with full, or nearly full, employment. In other words, implicit in the discussion up to now has been the assumption of continued prosperity. This appears reasonable, but it is only an assumption. A slowing down in the rate of total economic growth is a distinct possibility, and a major and prolonged economic depression is at least a possibility during the period.

[3] From a paper entitled "Adjusting the Structure of Agriculture to Economic Growth" presented before the North Central Farm Management Research Committee, Chicago, March 18–20, 1957. The full report of this major study is to be published by the National Planning Association.

An Analysis of Farm Price Behavior

The principal short-run effects on agriculture of a business depression are (1) a slowing down — and possibly even a contraction — of the rate of aggregate demand expansion, by reason of a decline in real personal incomes and (2) a drying up of job opportunities for surplus agriculture workers in the nonfarm sector. Both of these effects work in the direction of pushing down the farm price level. The longer run effects on agriculture of a general economic depression might be (1) a slowing down of the rate of population growth and (2) a slowing down of the rate of farm technological advance. These effects would tend to cancel each other out, but to what extent it is impossible to say.

One conclusion can be reached. An economic depression prior to 1975 would have the immediate effect of slowing down the rate of aggregate demand expansion *relative to* the rate of aggregate output expansion and hence act to drive farm prices to even lower levels than that indicated under continued prosperity. The farm price-income problem in the latter half of this century will be more than difficult to solve under conditions of prosperity; under depression conditions it would be impossible.

Market Organization and Technological Advance

Why in the face of falling farm prices and declining gross incomes do farmers persist in adopting new technologies, and thus expanding output? Why, in the 1950s, have farmers pushed aggregate output ahead of demand through widespread technological advance, and thus driven down the prices of their own products? And why are they likely to keep right on behaving in this seemingly irrational manner? In the main, the answer is to be found in the market organization of agriculture. But given this market organization, some other factors need to be considered: the role of society acting through government and the financial position of farmers. So let us inquire into the manner in which farmers adopt new technologies to see how and where they are led astray.

MARKET ORGANIZATION AND THE ADOPTION PROCESS

To this point farm technological advance has been considered in terms of the total agricultural industry — in terms of its shifting effects on the aggregate supply relation, hence upon the farm price level.[4] In this view,

[4] This section is adapted in part from W. W. Wilcox and Willard W. Cochrane, "Who Gets the Benefit of Farm Technological Advance," *Economics of American Agriculture* (New York: Prentice-Hall, 1951).

we see the effects on the industry of a particular technology or production practice *after it has been widely adopted throughout the industry.* If, however, we take as a unit of analysis not the industry but rather different firms in the dynamic process of adoption, the story changes. And this is what we shall do now: consider the effects of farm technological advance on firms that adopt the technique early, then on the more typical followers, and finally on the laggards.

It should be recognized, first, that farmers typically operate in a special sort of a market — one that satisfies the key conditions of a perfectly competitive market: namely, a market in which no one farmer can have, or does have, any perceptible influence on the price of his product (or his factors of production). The farmer is a price taker; he takes the price offered him because he is such a small part of the total market that he can have no perceptible influence on the market or on the market price.

Second, it will be recalled that a technological advance has the effect of lowering the *per unit costs of production* of the farm firm (typically, per unit costs of production are reduced as the total value product increases by more than the increase in total costs; it is extremely difficult to think of a new technology that does not increase output). This being the case, farm producers who adopt a new technology (e.g., growing hybrid seed corn) early in the game realize increased net returns from undertaking that enterprising act. The new technique reduces costs of production for the enterprising few, but they are such a small part of the market that total output is not increased noticeably and price does not come down. Net incomes of the few adopters are increased and a powerful incentive is created for other farmers to adopt the technique.

In this explanation we find the basis of continuing and widespread farm technological advance. The operators who first adopt a new technology reap the income benefits (the difference between the old price and the new, lower unit costs). Then other farmers in the community see the income advantage accruing to Mr. Early Bird; also, the Extension Service and other educational units spread the information around. So Mr. Average Farmer decides he will adopt this cost-reducing technique, and this includes most farmers in the community. *But the widespread adoption of this new technology changes the entire situation. Total output is now increased, and this increase in the supply of the commodity lowers the price of that commodity.* And where the price elasticity of demand at the farm level is less than —1.0 (i.e., demand is inelastic), as is commonly the case in agriculture, gross returns to the producers must fall. Further, over a period of time, any increases in net returns are capitalized back into the value of the land with the result that land prices rise.

As the dynamic process of technological adoption unfolds, we see two things happening: (1) in those cases in which the output of the commodity is increased, the price of the commodity falls relative to commodity substitutes; and (2) unit costs of production rise after their initial decline, as the gains from the new practice, or technique, are capitalized into the value of the fixed asset involved. So in the long run, by the time most farmers have adopted the technology, the income benefits that the first farmers realized have vanished. Mr. Average Farmer is right back where he started, as far as his income position is concerned. Once again, average unit costs of production are equal to price and no economic surplus remains.

If this is the typical result, why do farmers generally adopt new methods? It is easy to see why the first farmers undertake a new method or practice. They benefit directly. And we can understand why neighbors of the enterprising first farmers adopt the technology: they see the income advantage and make up their minds to give it a try. But, as more and more farmers adopt the new technology, output is affected and the price of the commodity declines. This price decline acts as a burr under the saddle of the followers, the average farmers; the price of their product is declining, but their unit costs of production are unchanged. *To stay even with the world these average farmers are forced to adopt the new technology.* The average farmer is on a treadmill with respect to technological advance.

In the quest for increased returns, or the minimization of losses, which the average farmer hopes to achieve through the adoption of some new technology, he runs faster and faster on the treadmill. But by running faster he does not reach the goal of increased returns; the treadmill simply turns over faster. And as the treadmill speeds up, it grinds out more and more farm products for consumers.

In a sympathetic book [5] in which Dale Kramer tells the story of the tides of agrarian revolt in the United States, he calls with a rough-and-ready sense of humor, those farmers in revolt the wild jackasses. Perhaps it is appropriate in this context to say that the many farmers running

---

[5] *The Wild Jackasses* (New York: Hasting House Publishers, 1956).

on the agricultural treadmill have been used as tame jackasses — as tame jackasses grinding out greater and greater supplies of food with no advantage, and perhaps with disadvantage, to themselves.

The position of the laggard, who will not or cannot adopt the new technologies, is a tragic one. The farmer who belongs to a religious sect that does not permit technological advance, the aged or beginning farmer who cannot afford the initial cost of the technology or production practice, or the lazy fellow who prefers to go fishing, finds himself in an income squeeze. The relative price of the commodity falls as one technique after another is adopted throughout the industry, but his unit costs of production do not come down. Thus, the farmer who does not adopt new technologies and practices is squeezed and squeezed. Farm technological advance for him is a nightmare.

In the preceding analysis, we reached the conclusion that any economic surplus growing out of the introduction of a new technology is squeezed to the zero point in the long run. But this does not mean that the labor income to operators and hired labor must fall, even when the price level is falling. We have yet to take up another dynamic consideration: the substitution of machinery and equipment for labor. Increased farm mechanization most often takes the form of substituting a machine process for a hand process. If in these situations gross returns are unaffected and total costs of the unit under consideration (the firm, or total agriculture) decline, then the labor income of those workers remaining *must* be increased.

In the more typical case in which output expands, demand is inelastic and gross revenue declines. If the impact of the new technology (e.g., the general purpose tractor and the variety of hookups) is such as to reduce the number of workers required in the industry, as well as to reduce total costs of production, the average labor income of those remaining *may not* decrease; or, if it does, it will not decrease as much as would otherwise be the case. In this situation, the average labor income of those remaining in agriculture develops into a three-cornered race between declining total revenue, declining total costs, and declining numbers of workers. No generalization can be made with respect to this race except to say that it probably operates to increase income disparities *within* agriculture: the labor income of the efficient producer, farming more land with more capital, holds constant or rises, and the labor income of average and poor farmers declines.

SOCIAL ACTION AND THE ADOPTION PROCESS

The typical small family farmer, of course, is not and has not been in a position to undertake the costly, time-consuming work of developing new technological practices for his farm operation. But the many small farmers who make up the agricultural industry have rarely organized to promote and finance research and development through their own private agencies. In fact — and even though farmers are notorious tinkerers — farm people have often displayed an antagonistic attitude toward scientific inquiry and development. In recent years they have come to accept and even rely on a continuing change in the state of the arts in agriculture, but in most instances they have not initiated those changes. Thus, we conclude that if the availability of new production practices and techniques for farm adoption were dependent upon farmers' initiative, such practices and techniques would have been in short supply for many years.

But new production practices and techniques for agriculture have not been in short supply; to the contrary, there has been a continuous outpouring of these new technologies in the twentieth century. And the most important reason why there has been this generous supply since the turn of the century is that society decided to take collective action to assure this ample supply of new technologies.

The nation established "agricultural and mechanical arts" colleges in the mid-nineteenth century to service the technological needs of agriculture. Society, acting through the federal government and the various state governments, has more than generously financed the research and development work in those colleges and in governmental research agencies ever since. This is not to say that every important technological development in agriculture has been the direct result of work in the land-grant colleges and governmental research agencies. Far from it: private agencies have contributed many new technologies for use in agriculture, and appear to be providing an increasing proportion. But it is to say that *society has covered the overhead costs of training scientists and carrying on the basic research which lies behind every applied technique.*

The point is that society has underwritten technological advance in agriculture by guaranteeing a continuous outpouring of new production techniques for adoption on farms. If farm technological advance does not outrace population growth in the period 1955–75, it won't be because the new techniques are not there to be adopted. By generously financing research and development in agricultural production, society has made as certain as possible that an ample outpouring of new techniques will continue.

This willingness of society to finance research and development in agricultural production is in many ways a strange phenomenon. Perhaps in some collective and intuitive sense society feels that a rapid rate of technological advance in agriculture is basic to rising levels of living for its members — as indeed it is. By underwriting a rapid rate of technological advance, society assures itself of a bountiful food supply at relatively low prices. But the strange aspect of all this is that this generous financing of research and development is all done in the name of helping farmers, and it is so accepted by most farmers and their leaders.

Now in the short-run monopoly sense, (i.e., the highwayman sense) nothing could be farther from the truth. The monopolist always seeks a position where his product is relatively scarce and the products of all other groups are plentiful; from this position of market power the monopolist trades scarce, dear items for cheap, plentiful items. But a rapid rate of technological advance — a rate of technological advance that drives aggregate supply ahead of aggregate demand — places the farmer in just the opposite position; places him in the weak market position of producing bountiful supplies at low prices.

FARMER ASSET POSITIONS AND THE ADOPTION PROCESS

In a free market at least, aggregate supply cannot outrace aggregate demand indefinitely. At some point in time, its pace must slow down and become equal to, or perhaps even lag behind, the rate of demand expansion. In other words, the expansion rates of these two relations are related; the connection is somewhat indirect, but it is there. The aggregate demand and the aggregate supply relations are related through the nexus of the asset positions of farmers.

Most new technologies adopted on farms are capital using — that is, their adoption requires an additional cash outlay or some kind of additional financial commitment. But since the adoption of a new technology reduces unit costs, farmers are willing to make the additional investments so long as they can. And they can so long as their liquid and capital asset positions are strong and unimpaired.

But these asset positions deteriorate under a falling farm price level

99

with the attendant declines in gross and net incomes. The liquid asset position typically goes first; but with the passage of time capital assets become encumbered in order to cope with losses resulting from declining incomes. In a free market situation, then, farm technological advance sows the seeds of its own slow-down. If aggregate output outraces aggregate demand long enough and far enough, and the farm price level falls far enough and stays down long enough, the asset position of farmers generally will become weak, and the process of farm adoption of new technologies must be choked off. In this way the rate of output expansion is slowed down and brought into equality with the rate of demand expansion.

This, of course, is a painful process, as farmers in a limited way have discovered in the 1950s. Furthermore, it is no simple process. The slowdown in farm technological advance will not be uniform. It will first strike the inefficient farmers and the beginners: the vulnerable asset positions of these farmers deteriorate rapidly when the farm price level declines. The average farmer will hold out longer, and the very efficient farmer succumbs to the slow-down only in extreme situations. The efficient farmer, the early adopter of new techniques, who reaps the income rewards accruing to him as such, and who successfully increases his labor income by substituting machinery and equipment for labor, can withstand and even thrive in a major price decline *to a point*.

It should be emphasized here, however, that the rate of output expansion, powered by farm technological advance, does not slow down immediately when it encounters a price level decline. Witness the rapid rate of output expansion in the early 1950s in the face of a falling farm price level. Farmers generally came out of the World War II period with strong asset positions and for this reason generally have been able to maintain a rapid rate of technological advance in the face of a falling price level. The rate of output expansion in the 1950s and 1960s will not slow down until the asset positions of these many average or representative farmers begin to be impaired. But in a free market situation the slow-down in the rate of aggregate output expansion must ultimately come, as the slow-down in the adoption of new technologies engulfs more and more farmers.

The question may be asked: Will the rate of aggregate output expansion be slowed down and become equal to the rate of demand expansion by 1975? The answer to that question must be: It depends upon the kinds of governmental action taken — upon the collective action of society. If farm prices and incomes are supported in some way, but production controls remain ineffective as in the past, then the answer is probably no. At the 1955 farm price level, with production controls no more effective than those in existence before 1955, the evidence suggests that aggregate output will continue to outdistance aggregate demand. But a return to a free market in agriculture and the lower level of farm prices that would be generated in a free market would probably lead to a decline in the rate of output expansion, and possible equality with the rate of demand expansion by 1975, via the nexus of farmers' asset positions.[6]

The way of agriculture may be hard, but it is not hopeless, as the above conclusions might imply. Those two policy alternatives do illustrate, however, the effect that farm asset positions generally may be expected to have on the rate of aggregate output expansion.

The Consequences of Farm Technological Advance

The spotlight in this section will be on the period 1920–55, the period in which total inputs employed in agriculture remained constant, and when increases in total output must therefore have resulted from new configurations in the use of productive resources (i.e., from technological advance). It will be recalled that total farm output increased throughout the nineteenth century and during the first two decades of the twentieth as the result of (1) an expansion in the size of the fixed plant of agriculture and (2) technological advance, with the former decreasing in importance and the latter increasing over the long period. Hence, it is difficult, if not impossible, to know what part of the increase in total output is attributable to technological advance and what part to an increase in the size of the fixed plant during that long period. But from 1920 to 1955 all, or practically all, of the increase in total marketable output must be attributed to technological advance. There is nothing else to attribute it to.[7]

[6] Countless alternatives falling between these extremes could be considered, and some of the better known ones will be considered in Chapters 7 and 8.

[7] It is sometimes argued that increases in total output between 1920 and 1955 may be attributed to farm firms' becoming more efficient (i.e., farmers were successful in locating and moving toward the minimum point of their long-run planning curves) over this long period. But this argument flies in the face of facts and logic. The state of the arts was changing over the entire period, sometimes slowly, sometimes rapidly. Farmers were continuously adjusting to new levels and patterns of

101

FOOD SUPPLY

The technological developments that occurred during the period 1920–55, and which were adopted on commercial farms during that period, enabled farmers to produce with the same total volume of resources a more than adequate food supply for the growing population. Thus, the first and most necessary goal of this and every society was achieved: an adequate food supply. Never before had it happened that an adequate food supply for an expanding population was provided without the employment of more total resources in agriculture. John M. Brewster sums up the consequences of farm technological advance for the food supply in these words: "For the first time in history, gain in labor productivity appreciably outraced the rate of population increase during the 20's and became four times faster during the 30's. For every 100 workers needed in agriculture in 1930, only 79 were needed in 1940. The pressure of population upon the food supply had done an about face." [8]

First through the beneficence of plentiful and fertile land resources and second because of technological advance, consumers in the United States enjoy a rich, varied, and, if they so choose, nutritious diet. This is a blessing that few people in the past have enjoyed, and that relatively few people in the world enjoy even today.

RELEASE OF HUMAN RESOURCES

Farm technological advance not only assures Americans of an adequate food supply in the 1950s, but over the years it has released millions of farm-reared people to work in manufacturing, in the distributive system, and in the arts, sciences, and professions. This, of course, is the mark of economic progress: first the release of workers from agriculture to go into manufacturing, and then the release of workers from both of these categories to enter the service trades (and to enjoy increased leisure time) *as the real incomes of all continue to rise.*

The process by which these people have been released from agriculture has not always been a kindly one, but it has taken place. It has

---

technology over the entire period. By what logic then can one argue that farmers were more nearly at the minimum point of their long-run static cost curves in 1955, than farmers were in 1920? None, except by assertion. The facts are that farmers were adjusting to new technologies over the entire period, not seeking minimum points on *static* planning curves.

[8] "Farm Technological Advance and Total Population Growth," *Journal of Farm Economics*, August 1945, p. 515.

happened as workers in agriculture have become increasingly productive — as one worker, armed with new production techniques, has been able to produce enough food and fiber to meet the wants of more and more nonfarm people. To illustrate: in 1820 one worker in agriculture could support 4.12 persons including himself and by 1920 one worker could support 8.27 persons; but by 1955 one worker in agriculture could support 19.74 persons. In other words, the capacity of an agricultural worker to feed and clothe people doubled in the first 100 years, but more than doubled in the next 35 years.

The proportion of the total labor force of the United States employed in agriculture has declined steadily over the long-run past: from 72 per cent in 1820 to 18 per cent in 1920 to about 10 per cent in 1955. This is common knowledge. But not so generally known is the fact that total employment in agriculture reached a peak of 13.6 million workers in 1910 and has been declining ever since. Further, the movement of labor resources out of agriculture has been rapid in recent years: total employment in agriculture fell from 11 million persons in 1940 to 9.3 million in 1950 and to 8.2 million in 1955. This is no small decline.

Since 1920 the substitution of machines for men in agriculture has been rapid indeed. Where this process of substitution will end no one knows, but it is reworking the face of agriculture in the 1950s, increasing the average size of farms (in acres), greatly increasing the capital investment on farms, and commercializing the farm operation. And the substitution of machines for men may reorganize the family farm out of existence in years to come.

FARMERS' INCENTIVE INCOMES

Incentive income is a concept developed by J. R. Bellerby to describe the return to human effort and enterprise.[9] In farming this is the return to the farmer as a manager, laborer, and technician. It does not include any return to property or capital. The income incentive ratio relates the incentive income of farmers on a per man unit basis to the incentive income of persons engaged in nonfarm enterprises on a per man unit basis. The incentive income ratio, thus, compares the average, or per unit, return to human effort and enterprise on the two sides of the farm-nonfarm fence. By five-year intervals, the farm-nonfarm incentive income ratio for the interwar period is as follows: [10]

[9] *Agriculture and Industry Relative Income* (New York: Macmillan, 1956), p. 16.
[10] Bellerby, *op. cit.*, p. 187.

103

1920	46
1925	38
1930	32
1935	43
1940	32

During the interwar period the incentive income of farmers is consistently less than 50 per cent of nonfarm incentive incomes. In other words, when only the returns to human effort and enterprise are considered (i.e., when the returns to capital are excluded), the returns to farmers as compared with nonfarm workers are shockingly low.

It is interesting to note that Bellerby computed these incentive income ratios for many countries for the interwar period, and that the United States falls near the bottom of the list. The incentive income ratio is higher for all the following countries than for the United States: Australia, New Zealand, France, United Kingdom, Denmark, Sweden, and Canada. The incentive income ratio of the United States exceeds that of only a few underdeveloped countries — Egypt, Mexico, and Thailand, for example.[11]

As we have observed, widespread technological advance on farms in the United States since 1920 has assured the growing population of the United States of an adequate food supply and gives promise of underwriting an adequate food supply in the foreseeable future. Widespread farm technological advance has also released several million agricultural workers for nonfarm employment, and gives promise of releasing many more in the foreseeable future. But widespread farm technological advance during the interwar period did not result in high incentive incomes for farmers relative to nonfarm workers. It contributed to low incentive incomes for farmers, as farm technological advance first expanded aggregate output, and then sustained aggregate output in the face of a contraction in aggregate demand during the Great Depression. In the United States, then, where farm technological advance was the most rapid in the world during the interwar period, the incentive income ratio was among the lowest in the world.

Immediately following World War II, when the United States made some effort to feed the hungry, famine-ridden peoples of Europe and the Far East, the income incentive ratio rose to the 50 per cent level. But with falling gross and net farm incomes in the 1950s resulting from

[11] *Ibid.*, p. 270.

the falling farm price level which resulted, in turn, from aggregate output marching ahead of aggregate demand again, the incentive income ratio fell back to the levels of the depressed 1930s. The incentive income ratio is given below for selected years: [12]

$$1947\ldots\ldots\ldots\ldots\ldots\ 50$$
$$1950\ldots\ldots\ldots\ldots\ldots\ 44$$
$$1955\ldots\ldots\ldots\ldots\ldots\ 30$$

Truly, the American farmer is on a treadmill. On it he is running faster and faster in the quest for higher incomes growing out of the adoption of new and more productive techniques, but he is not gaining incomewise. *He is losing.*

The General Theory of the Agricultural Treadmill

The capacity of American farmers to command good and stable prices and incomes in the market is weak; the power position of farmers in the market is weak. The farmer *takes* the prices that the market offers him, and very often these are low prices.

The farmer's weak position in the market (i.e., the low prices offered him, and his inability to reject those low prices and command higher ones) grows out of three related circumstances: first, the high value that American society generally places on technological development and application; second, the market organization within which farmers operate; and third, the extreme inelasticity of the aggregate demand for food. The combination of these circumstances places farmers in an unenviable position.

The American people have not singled out agriculture to carry the burden of technological advance; Americans prize technological advance highly, expect it, and demand it in all segments of the economy. As Bushrod W. Allin stated in the 1957 Lecture Series of the Graduate School of the United States Department of Agriculture, *belief in technology* is a part of the American creed: [13] The "dynamics in American culture I shall call the American creed — a blend that is peculiarly American. The three principal dynamics of this creed are:

[12] Not given by Bellerby for the postwar period, but estimated here by the procedures outlined by him in *Agriculture and Industry Relative Income*, pp. 187–189. See Appendix Tables 3 and 4 of this volume for data and computations relating to these postwar estimates.

[13] "Rural Influences on the American Politico-Economic System," lecture before the U.S. Department of Agriculture Graduate School, April 1957.

(1) Belief in enterprise
(2) Belief in democracy
(3) Belief in technology."

This belief in technology Americans are willing to back with dollars — in fact with 7 billion of them in 1956.[14] With few exceptions, businessmen believe that it is good business to develop new and better products, and to this end they spend vast sums in research and development. In fact, competition in the nonfarm sector commonly takes the form of product competition; in this common situation firms do not compete through price; they compete through product differentiation — by means of an improved product, or a different product. As we have already noted, society has been generous in the financing of research and development in agriculture. Our society expects a rapid rate of technological development, and it has experienced a rapid rate of technological advance in most lines of endeavor, including agriculture.

The farmer operates in a sea of competitive behavior; each farmer is a tiny speck on this sea and the output of each farmer is a tiny drop in this sea. With rare exceptions, the single farmer operates in a market so large, that he can have no perceptible influence on it. In this situation, the farmer must take as given to him the prices generated in the market.

Confronted with this situation, he reasons "I can't influence price, but I can influence my own costs. I can get my costs down." So the typical farmer is always searching for some way to get his costs down. By definition a new technology is cost reducing (i.e., it increases output per unit of input). Thus, the farmer is always on the lookout for new, cost-reducing technologies. Built into the market organization of agriculture, then, is a powerful incentive for adopting new technologies — the incentive of reducing costs on the individual farm.

Now if the demand for food were highly elastic all would be sweetness and light in agriculture. If the aggregate demand for food were *elastic*, the bountiful and expanding supplies of food that farmers want to produce would sell in the market at only slightly reduced prices and gross incomes to farmers, in the aggregate and individually, would increase. But the aggregate demand for food is not elastic; it is inelastic and extremely so. For this reason, a little too much in the way of total output drives down the farm price level in a dramatic fashion, and reduces

---

[14] Report to Congress from the *Commission on Increased Industrial Uses of Agricultural Products*, Senate Document No. 45, 85th Congress, 1st session, June 1957.

106

the gross incomes of farmers in a similar fashion. Furthermore, the persistent pressure on each farmer to adopt new technologies and thereby reduce unit costs has the effect of continuously putting a little too much in the way of supplies on the market. The peacetime tendency for aggregate supply to outrace aggregate demand keeps farm prices relatively low.

A general theory of the agricultural treadmill has been sketched. The high value that society places on technological advance guarantees a continuous outpouring of new technologies. The incentive to reduce costs on the many, many small farms across the country guarantees a rapid and widespread adoption of the new technologies. Rapid and widespread farm technological advance drives the aggregate supply relation ahead of the expanding aggregate demand relation in peacetime; and, given the highly inelastic demand for food, farm prices fall to low levels and stay there for long periods.

PART III

Economics and Policy

6

The Economist as a Policy Adviser

The problems isolated in Part I were economic in nature; economic data, prices, and incomes were involved and the problems resulted from the failure of the agricultural economy to provide reasonably good and stable prices and incomes. Similarly, the analyses in Part II were economic in nature; economic data, prices, incomes, and supplies were involved and various relationships involving prices and quantities were formulated and presented to explain the workings of the agricultural economy. The economic analyses of Part II were designed to throw light on the economic problems of Part I. Thus, common sense would suggest that an economist should be called in to prescribe what *ought* to be done about these problems (i.e., what courses of action *should* be followed to correct the problematic situations). This is a role in which the agricultural economist commonly finds himself; he isolates and defines a problem, he studies it and develops an analysis of the problematic situation, and then the persons involved — farmers or middlemen or politicians — call on him to advise on the formulation of a course of action to correct the situation.

Now this is flattering to the agricultural economist and generally he comes forward with the sought-after advice. It may well be, as will be argued later, that agricultural economists hold a preferred or strategic position among technical agriculturists for giving advice on policy questions. But this strategic position does not stem exclusively, or even most importantly, from a knowledge of economic relations (although such knowledge is useful in describing the economic consequences of alternative courses of action). Basically it stems from the know-how of economists with respect to socio-politico-economic processes.

If, then, it is correct that the advice of agricultural economists on policy questions arising out of economic problems is not generally sought because of their knowledge of economic relationships, but rather for their abilities as "generalists," how does the economist operate in this policy field, what are the relations of economic analysis to policy formulation, and of economists to policy making? A discussion of these questions should prove helpful to laymen who often seek the counsel of economists on policy matters, and to economists who don't always seem to understand the role they are playing in policy making.

Economics and Policy

Economics is not a synonym for policy, or policy for economics. The principles of economics, which must be the propositions or conclusions deduced from the abstract logic of economics, are not and cannot be the principles of policy or policy making (although some economists new to politics must think that they are, since they deride any aspect of policy not consistent with their set of economic principles as *politics*). Policy is broader and more inclusive than economics, whether economics be defined in the narrow sense of efficiency (i.e., the efficient use of resources), or in the broader sense of institutions, development, and income and employment, as well as efficiency.

Policy may be defined as the conscious and purposive pursuit of a course of action by a decision unit (e.g., household, firm, voluntary association, or government) to realize some goal, or a set of goals; the pursuit of this course of action has implications or consequences in various, usually many, fields of human activity. Conventionally, however, the term policy — unless modified in some way (e.g., "firm" policy) — refers to a course of action by government; the term will be used in this restricted sense in this chapter. By policy we will mean a course of action taken by government which has implications or consequences in a myriad of areas: economic efficiency, economic growth and development, size of the national income, income distribution, the various social institutions (the family, the family-sized farm, the public school system, churches), the conservation of resources, national defense, the availability of medical care, scientific research and development, the physical protection of workers, the psychic well-being of members of a community, and so on. Every course of action will not touch every field of human activity, but every course of action will touch many fields.

Important to this discussion, a specific policy will have implications in many fields of human activity; hence its implications require study, analysis, and consideration in the many fields involved. As regards inclusiveness, it makes little difference whether a course of action is undertaken to correct an economic problem such as that posed by low farm incomes, or to deal with such a health problem as providing more medical care at less cost. The course of action concerned with an economic problem will have social, aesthetic, and institutional implications as well as economic. The course of action taken to deal with a health problem will have resource allocation and income distribution implications as well as technical medical implications. The first point on which we should be clear is this: a course of action embarked upon by society to deal with a specific problematic situation — low farm incomes, a scarcity of teachers, an inadequate air force — will have implications, and perhaps its most important implications, outside the immediate field of activity.

Policy-making processes also differ in form and procedure from economizing processes. In policy making, the decision unit, whether at the family level or the federal government level, seeks to formulate with respect to *a particular problem* a course of action which yields results in the many fields of human activities touched upon, which best satisfies the decision unit with respect to the totality of human activities. Making policy thus means effecting compromises among competing ends. To get the kind of results wanted in one field, and to avoid certain results in another field, the decision unit may be forced to accept less than desired results in some third and perhaps fourth fields. This is what policy formation is all about: the compromising of one goal to realize more of whatever is involved in some other goals and thus to increase the total satisfaction of the persons involved. Compromise is the very essence of policy making.

The process of economizing, on the other hand, has but one goal. Given prices and the state of the arts, the minimum cost, or maximum profit, position (under competitive conditions these two positions are identical) of the firm is uniquely determinable. And given the tastes and preferences of society and the state of the arts, the optimum combination of resources in terms of maximizing the total utility of society is uniquely determinable. There is no compromise in the economizing process. The decision-making unit has one goal: maximizing output in terms of inputs, and a unique solution to this goal may be found.

113

Consequently the analytical methods used in studying and explaining policy making on the one hand and economizing on the other should and do differ. In the latter case, rigorous, mathematical methods, capable of yielding unique solutions, are used. In the former case, the methods commonly used are less precise and more varied, often running in psychological terms. It is difficult to develop tight, logical arguments to describe the art of compromise; hence discussions of policy making tend to be newsy, emphasizing personalities and pressure group tactics. More profound discussions of policy move into the area of human valuations: the evolution of values and the examination of values and valuation conflicts.[1] It is at this level that analyses of policy become fruitful, for it is at this level that the crucial decisions and basic conflicts in policy making occur.

Human Values and Policy

How do such decision units as the proprietor of a small business (say, an automobile sales agency), the management of a large corporation (say, U.S. Steel), the individual family, and the federal government effect compromises and arrive at an economic policy? They do it in accordance with the value, the worth, which they attach to the results that are likely to obtain in different areas of human activity from alternative courses of action. They seek a particular course of action which yields results that are highly valued, and try to avoid results that are negatively valued.

In the case of a small business firm operating in a competitive situation, the formulation of economic policy is usually relatively easy; the desire to maximize profits overrides all other objectives; it is the result *valued* above all others. Given this highly prized objective, plus the competitive condition wherein the profit-maximizing position of the firm is also the cost-minimizing position, the formulation of policy be-

[1] As Gunnar Myrdal points out in his important work *An American Dilemma: The Negro Problem and Modern Democracy* (New York: Harper and Brothers, 1944), the term value is used loosely and ambiguously on many occasions; hence he uses the term valuation in place of value. But this does not seem to solve the terminological problem. By *value* we mean the *worth* that a person attaches to an object, act, or idea — the degree to which a person cherishes, or prizes, an object, act, or idea. And the meaning remains the same whether the thing being valued is made explicit, or the term value is used to connote both the worth of a thing and the thing itself. The term *valuation* is used here to refer to the process whereby the worth of a thing is established. The term *evaluation* is used here to indicate the value of one item in comparison with another; it involves a comparison of values.

comes perfectly straightforward. The firm will pursue that course of action that yields the greatest profits.

At the level of a large corporation like U.S. Steel, the formulation of economic policy becomes more complex. The objective of profit maximization continues to be highly valued, but other objectives — and not necessarily parallel ones — are valued too. The cost-minimization position of a great business corporation is no longer identical with its profit-maximization position, and it may seek a low cost-profit position to forestall the entry of competing firms. There is the question of time, too; the firm may, for example, elect to pursue an investment policy which lowers profits in the short run, but which is intended to maximize profits over the longer run. It may also want to avoid becoming as large as the maximum profit position might dictate (by reason of the increased bargaining strength that goes with increased size), because government would enter the picture with an anti-monopoly policy. And it might, for humanitarian reasons, want to develop good housing conditions, good retirement schemes, and vacation plans for its employees. Now the above goals, which are valued by management, are to some degree in conflict with one another. How they will be resolved, or compromised, to construct a general economic policy for the corporation will depend upon the value, the worth, placed upon each of these goals by management.

At the level of the single family the process of policy formulation becomes increasingly complex — so complex, in fact, that few if any families have *an* economic policy. The father may value a job highly for the peace of mind it provides, whereas his wife attaches a low value to it because it pays a low wage. The father may want to rent an apartment near his work, his wife want a rambler in the suburbs, and the children want an old house in the country. So the wants and valuation conflicts of this family multiply with regard to sources of income and items of expenditure. But from coalitions of agreements on the value of this item of expenditure or that source of income, short-run economic policies or courses of action emerge within families. These policies often are not consistent one with another; they are formed, go to pieces, and are re-formed in the typical family as personal values change with the life cycle of the family. In sum, out of values held in common, families develop short-run income and expenditure policies; but these policies are tenuous and transitory, because different members of a family value

115

the receipt and expenditure of income differently, and the values of each family member change with age and growth.

Policy formulation at the federal government level encounters all those complexities found in the family, plus some additional ones. In a sense the national society is the family society *writ large*. But the diffused members of the national society may be expected to have less homogeneous value systems than those of a typical family. Further, because of the large numbers of people involved in the national society, the means for effecting compromises and agreement are necessarily more complex. Thus, we do not find *an* economic policy at the federal level. Views of what government should and should not do are too varied, judgments concerning what constitutes desirable and undesirable economic behavior are too varied, and goals for the development of the economic society are too varied at the national level to admit of *an* economic policy.

But policies are formulated and pursued at the national level with respect to *specific economic problems* like unemployment or low farm income. These policies emerge within the Congress and the administration of the federal government as areas of agreement are discovered, or are formed, in the national society with respect to the facts of a problematic situation and what ought to be done about it. The existence of a cultural unity, or the establishment of a unity, with regard to the facts of a problematic situation and human values, provides an indispensable basis for group discussion and action. It is the common ground on which policies are forged.

The content of national policies (i.e., the *nature* of a course of action) depends upon the valuations made by society of the results of alternative courses of action in different fields of human activity, and the valuation conflicts arising out of differently valued results in different fields of human activity. Myrdal puts it this way:

. . . *As people's valuations are conflicting, behavior normally becomes a moral compromise. There are no homogeneous "attitudes" behind human behavior but a mesh of struggling inclinations, interests, and ideals, some held conscious and some suppressed for long intervals but all active in bending behavior in their direction.*[2]

In place of "behavior," read "course of action," and this quotation is directly applicable to the present discussion.

[2] *Ibid.*, p. xlviii.

Policy formulation by the national society thus involves compromise at two levels: (1) compromise among individuals regarding the value or worth of the result of a policy in *one* field of human activity (arriving at a general agreement, or cultural unity, among members of society with regard to the worthwhileness of a specific policy result), and (2) compromise by society, as in the case of the individual, among differently valued results in different fields of human activity from a given course of action (for society to acquire the results in one field of human activity which are valued highly, certain results in other fields, valued less highly, must be foregone). Compromise at the first level establishes a community of interest for group action; compromise at the second establishes the content of the group action, i.e., the policy.

To inquire further into the question of values and policy, let us ignore for the moment the problem of heterogeneous value systems among members of the national society, and assume that society shares the following system of values. It prizes, or values highly, these attributes:

1. Efficiency (i.e., the maximization of output per unit of input).

2. Individualism (i.e., the maximization of the area of individual decision making).

And it is indifferent to, or values slightly, these attributes:

1. Custom and established traditions.

2. The protection of individuals in terms of socially accepted income, consumption, and other living norms (i.e., the avoidance of inequitable situations).

A society with this system of values is likely to develop a price and income policy for agriculture that involves little or no collective action to control supplies, support prices, supplement farm incomes, or subsidize the increased consumption of food. This conclusion follows from the following facts. First, collective or governmental action to control supplies and support prices and incomes would obviously violate the highly valued goal of individualism by narrowing the economic decision area of farmers. Second, positive governmental action to control supply and thereby support prices and incomes would lead to certain resource allocation problems and short-run inefficiencies.[3] Third, a society that was indifferent to the income problems of its individual members would cer-

[3] In the longer run such a governmental action designed to support prices and incomes might lead to increased efficiency as increased stability induced a faster rate of capital formation and hastened the adoption of new technological methods in agriculture.

tainly not compromise its highly valued goals of efficiency and individualism to deal with a low income problem in agriculture.

Let us assume, on the other hand, that a society shares the following system of values. It prizes, or values highly, these attributes:

1. The protection of individuals in terms of socially accepted income, consumption, and other living norms (i.e., the avoidance of inequitable situations).

2. The concept and practice of the family farm.

And it is indifferent toward these attributes:

1. Increased governmental controls over economic decision making.

2. Efficiency (i.e., the maximization of output per unit of input).

Such a society is likely to develop a price and income policy for agriculture involving considerable collective action to control supplies, support prices, supplement farm incomes, and subsidize the increased consumption of food. In the first place there is the obvious fact that this society would want to — would feel compelled to — do something about low or unstable incomes in agriculture. Second, more government activity in the economic sector would not disturb members of this society. Third, this society is indifferent to the resource allocation problem; it is more concerned with equity problems than it is with efficiency problems.

The way the above valuation problems were set up, the policy solution for each system of values was obvious. The necessity for compromise among individuals was obviated by assuming homogeneous value systems; the necessity for compromise among competing ends was obviated by establishing an internally consistent and conveniently scaled system of values. But the actual valuation problem with respect to American agriculture as of the 1950s is not so simple. The two different value systems outlined above are partly in conflict and partly intertwined in the current American experience. Where the conflicting value systems are intertwined in the same person, and this is most common, that person is badly mixed up — riding in one direction on one occasion and in another on another occasion. Where those systems are intertwined by reason of being held by different persons and groups, heated controversy and power struggles are the result.

Americans of the 1950s are thoroughly confused about what is good and what is bad for agriculture. Those broad areas of agreement *among* Americans with respect to the facts of the case in agriculture and a set of values for agriculture have not emerged as a basis for collective action. Nor has there emerged an internally consistent set of values leading to the selection of an economic policy for agriculture which yields generally accepted results in all fields of human activity. Hence an effective, generally acceptable price and income policy for agriculture has not emerged.

To sum up, policies are not constructed out of principles, relationships, or facts. Principles, relationships, and facts have a role to play in making clear what the consequences of a particular course of action may be and hence in contributing to rational decision making; but principles, relationships, and facts are not the stuff out of which policy is made. Very simply, policies are formulated and pursued to yield results that are highly valued, and to avoid results that are negatively valued. Policies become sharp and clear when human values are internally consistent, firmly held, and widely shared; policies change as human value systems change. Limitation of resources, physical conditions, and human behavior may place restraints on the formulation and execution of policy, but basically *policy grows out of what people want,* not out of physical forces or economic principles.

If society wants to run water uphill, and it understands the implications of and consequences of running water uphill, it can formulate a course of action designed to pump it uphill. Similarly, society can and does pursue "unnatural" courses of action with respect to prices and incomes. Society gets into trouble with respect to price and income policies designed to yield results other than those that obtain in the market place because it does not fully understand and appreciate the nature of the forces and relationships involved, and because different members of society value the consequences in different fields of human activity differently. But the point on which laymen and economists need to be clear is that in a democracy what people want in the way of a policy with respect to a problematic situation does and should determine, subject to certain constraints, what kind of a policy those people get; and what they want depends in turn on the valuations made by members of society with respect to the results, or consequences, of alternative courses of action.

The Economist and Policy Making

The discussion in the preceding two sections seems to suggest that the economist, in this case the agricultural economist, does not play a unique role in policy making. It was first pointed out that the implications or consequences of a particular course of action fan out into many fields of human activity; even a course of action designed to deal with an economic problem will have consequences to be considered outside the field of economics. It was pointed out secondly that the content of a particular course of action will depend on valuations made by the decision makers with respect to the possible and varied consequences of alternative courses of action. Thus, much of policy making seems to lie outside the provinces traditionally claimed and worked by economists.

This is the position held by many economists in recent years.[4] Men of this persuasion argue that the proper function of an economist is that of conceptualizing relationships among economic variables, and measuring or estimating these relationships. Such men are inclined to take a rather narrow view of economics (i.e., of the variables considered to be economic in nature). They tend to include within economics first and foremost those activities concerned with resource allocation — with the use of a given set of resources to maximize the total utility of society; and secondly and begrudgingly, the level of employment or size of the national income. But when, these moderns argue, the ideas developed by economists from a study of the above areas are *used* by economists to achieve some purpose, the men involved cease to be economists. When economists make value judgments, they have become businessmen, or reformers, or conservatives, or proponents of something; they have dropped their scientific role of describing and analyzing what is, and have assumed the role of partisans concerned with what ought to be. This, they argue, a man can and should do as a citizen, but should not and cannot do as a scientist.

The logic of this position seems unassailable. But this may be another case in which logic spun too finely has led men astray. Where followed, this logic leads economists to positions of social sterility, to the empty conclusion of modern welfare economics that "welfare increases whenever one or more individuals become more satisfied without any other individual's becoming less satisfied."[5] Further, many of these purists

---

[4] Following the lead of Lionel Robbins in his *Essay on the Nature and Significance of Economic Science* (London: Macmillan, 1932), most economists trained in the equilibrium tradition accept the view that economists cannot make policy recommendations without losing their status as economists and passing over into the realm of ethics. And modern "welfare economists" such as J. R. Hicks, N. Kaldor, M. W. Reder, and O. H. Brownlee avoid value judgments like the plague.

[5] M. W. Reder, *Studies in the Theory of Welfare Economics* (New York: Columbia University Press, 1947), p. 14.

have deluded themselves about the objectivity or neutrality of their analytical methods and theoretical systems. Professor Walker concludes, with respect to the neutrality of modern economic science:

This change in the attitude of many economists to the conventional objective of maximum satisfaction reflects the progressive nature of the movement toward a neutral economic theory, from which ethical precepts are excluded. When the movement began, the positive and normative elements in economic doctrine were thoroughly confused, and the first attempts to separate them were only partly successful. Some of the propositions which earlier economists accepted as positive statements are now seen to contain tacit value judgments and must therefore be transferred to the category of normative propositions. Assuming that different methods are appropriate to the positive study of things as they are and the choice of objectives, it would seem desirable to continue the scrutiny of all supposedly positive statements, with a view to weeding out any other unsuspected normative elements in economic theory. . . .

As it stands today, however, the body of doctrine which is usually taught as economic theory is only superficially neutral. Upon examination it will be found to owe its own form largely to value judgments as to what is desirable; and many of its verbally positive analyses carry normative force in practice. It may also be argued that academic teaching of conventional theory, despite and to some extent because of its apparent "impartiality," helps to train the moral sensibility of pupils in a particular direction.[6]

The position held by some economists that they are being "scientific" when they take human and social goals or ends as given, and advise decision-making units with respect to the best means of achieving such goals, is superficial indeed. As Kenneth H. Parsons has said, "What economists call ends do not operate in thought as targets do in archery. . . ."[7] Human values are an inextricable part of social action; they are principles of action, directing action but in turn influenced and modified by that action. Ends suggest means, means modify ends; therefore modified ends suggest modified means. This ends-means relation is a continuum in which ends are continuously reconstructed in the action process. Thus when economists say that they will advise on means, but not on ends, they take a mighty slippery position.

[6] E. Ronald Walker, *From Economic Theory to Policy* (Chicago: The University of Chicago Press, 1943), p. 213.

[7] "The Value Problem in Agricultural Policy," a paper given before the North Central Farm Management Research Committee, Chicago, March 18–21, 1957.

Economics and Policy

It might be well for modern economists to pay some attention to modern scientific method. The late Professor Mead once summed up the modern conception of the scientific method as follows:

. . . This modern conception proceeds from the standpoint not of formulating values, but giving society at the moment the largest possible number of alternatives of conduct, i.e., undertaking to fix from moment to moment the widest possible field of conduct. The purposes of conduct are to be determined in the presence of a field of alternative possibilities of action. The ends of conduct are not to be determined in advance, but in view of the interests that fuller knowledge of conditions awaken. . . .

We postulate freedom of action as the condition of formulating the ends toward which our conduct shall be directed. Ancient thought assured itself of its ends of conduct and allowed these to determine the world which tested its hypothesis. We insist such ends may not be formulated until we know the field of possible action. The formulation of the ends is essentially a social undertaking and seems to follow the statement of the field of possible conduct, while in fact the statement of the possible field of conduct is actually dependent on the push toward action. A moving end which is continually reconstructing itself follows upon the continually enlarging field of opportunities of conduct.[8]

In the everyday world of earning a living, business and labor power struggles, and politics, most economists do not, however, remain purists, pursuing at all times an objective, non-normative economic logic; they do not because they cannot. Society, which pays the bill, forces those who have been even modestly successful in unraveling the workings of the economy to participate in operating it. Society demands that the special knowledge acquired by economists concerning the workings of the economy be brought to bear on problematic situations by those same economists to help develop correctives for those situations. In other words, economists are forced to help formulate policy.

Now it will be argued here that economists generally, and agricultural economists in particular, may participate effectively and with propriety in policy making in two different ways. First, by tracing out the *economic* consequences that flow from a particular course of action, or from alternative courses of action. Second, by aspiring to and becoming general social scientists capable of (a) pointing out to individual members of society the consequences of a particular course of action in different fields of human activity, (b) examining received value systems

---

[8] From an essay by George H. Mead, "Scientific Method and Individual Thinker," in *Creative Intelligence: Essays in the Pragmatic Attitude* (New York: Henry Holt, 1917), pp. 223–224.

for consistency and purpose, conflicts among individuals and groups, and the development of those values, and (c) appraising the importance of the consequences of a course of action in all different fields in one complete, encompassing analysis. Each approach enables the economist to bring to the policy-making process some of the skills of his profession — analytical techniques and systematized knowledge. Well done, each approach can contribute importantly to the decision making of the average citizen unused to dealing with complex social problems. Poorly done, each approach can lead to either terrifying or amusing results.

Most economists prefer the first approach in dealing with policy problems, namely, the spelling out of *economic* consequences of alternative courses of action. To some degree the economist avoids the value problem — the making of value judgments and the influencing of other people's values — by this approach. He simply describes the results of alternative courses of action; he does not say which is better, or best. He does not, however, entirely escape the value problem by this approach; actually he makes judgments when he selects a particular course of action to study, and the conclusions he reaches concerning *economic consequences* imply standards, hence judgment. Most important, the analysis of alternative courses of action will, *if successful,* widen the field of possible conduct for many, and ultimately influence and modify their value systems. As the field of possible conduct (i.e., possible courses of action) widens as the result of research and inquiry, human horizons are widened and value systems change.

But the economist prefers this approach for other reasons. It is a research approach. He can study cause and effect relationships, and use many of the analytical concepts — demand relations, for example — developed within the discipline of economics. He feels at home in this approach; granted the orientation is different, but once under way the methods used are the old familiar methods.

Some agricultural economists have become unusually adept at this approach.[9] In advising on policy, they refrain from discussing the worthwhileness of a given course of action, or comparing the worthwhileness

[9] J. Carroll Bottom of Purdue University can discuss farm policy with Indiana farmers without generating heated controversies, but still impart enthusiasm and interest. And O. V. Wells of the U.S. Department of Agriculture has served as a major policy adviser to at least three administrations and maintained the good will and respect of all three by limiting his advice to what will be the economic consequences of a particular course of action.

of alternative courses of action, and the successful ones avoid with consummate skill value-laden words and phrases. They try to say only what a particular course of action, or alternative courses of action, will *do*. Usually practitioners of this approach present estimates of the price-quantity-income-cost results of one course of action as compared with others. The government economist typically *advises* policy-making officials on farm price and income policy by providing estimates of the price, cost, or income effects of alternative courses of action.

To illustrate, two government economists,[10] in a recent analysis of alternative pricing policies for wheat, estimated that the price of wheat per bushel as of 1956 would be $1.65 with no price-supporting operation but with government stocks at the beginning of the marketing year impounded; 88 cents with free markets, no restrictions on exports and government stocks not impounded; and 56 cents with free markets, exports limited to 400 million bushels, and government stocks not impounded. From information such as this, policy-making officials are able to predict something about the economic consequences of their acts. From information such as this, extension economists are able to explain to farmers the price effects and the control implications of alternative means of supporting farm incomes. In this manner economists help nonprofessional decision units to formulate a policy that yields the kind of results that those decision-makers had in mind in the first place. This kind of policy research helps decision-makers act rationally.

What about the implications or conseqences of one course of action as compared with another in fields other than economics? Won't decision units want information concerning the consequences of alternative courses of action in fields other than economics, too? The answer is yes in most cases. But at this level of consideration the economist cannot be scored for providing information in his field even though it is missing in other fields. He is open to criticism, however, if he says or leaves the impression that only economic consequences need to be considered, or that policy should be made consistent with economic principles, particularly efficiency principles, without regard to other social goals. All too often agricultural economists have taken such a myopic view in discussing price and income policy for agriculture.

[10] Richard J. Foote and Hyman Weingarten, "How Research Results Can Be Used to Analyze Alternative Government Policies," *Agricultural Economics Research*, U.S. Department of Agriculture, April 1956.

It is true, however, that farmers will always be vitally interested in the price-cost results of a farm policy, for these results influence or determine their incomes, hence their equity position in society. Nonfarm people are vitally interested in program costs and supply results of a farm policy, for these results influence their incomes too — also their food supply. Farm people and nonfarm people alike will almost always want economic analyses of farm policies. The income and supply implications of farm policies are so important to all members of society that economists are invariably called upon to describe these implications to lay decision-makers. But economists, and agricultural economists in particular, get into trouble when they assume either through ignorance or arrogance that policy consequences in other fields of human activity don't matter (i.e., that economics is synonymous with policy).

In the second general approach to policy participation, economists have the opportunity of contributing more directly to policy decisions — and of living more dangerously. To avail himself of this opportunity, or one might argue, duty, the economist must rise above the confining limits of economics and become in fact a social scientist; for, at the decision level, policy involves many aspects of human activity, not just the economic slice of it.[11]

At this level the *social scientist* can help the lay decision-maker in several ways. First, by pointing out the consequences of a course of action in all the different fields of human activity affected, the social scientist can help make clear and explicit the basic decision problem confronting decision units. This is most important to rational policy making, because the lay decision-maker, the citizen, with his limited experience and advice from specialists, usually sees only a part of the problem on which he is to make a decision, not the whole problem.

Second, by examining the received value systems of members of society for consistency and purpose, conflicts and development, the social scientist can help the layman understand why he acts as he does. When the layman knows what he values — what his system of values is like — he is in a position to consider and make changes in the most funda-

[11] This opportunity, or duty, is, of course, open to all professional men — the engineer, the medical doctor, the rural sociologist, the lawyer, and so on. It may be that the sociologist and lawyer come closer to performing as social scientists in their everyday work than do economists. But the fact remains that economists, particularly agricultural economists, often get pulled into policy formulation; hence they should consider this second approach.

mental aspects of himself: his values. This kind of work is usually upsetting, for human values under close examination often appear irrational, inconsistent, and archaic. *But this kind of work must be undertaken if we are to understand policy formation, for here we find the well-springs, the motivations, of policy.*

Third, by appraising the importance of policy results in different fields, the social scientist provides lay decision-makers with one reasoned analysis, considering all facets of the problem, which leads to a conclusion regarding the desirability or worthwhileness of one course of action relative to others. Decision units need not accept all, or any part, of such an analysis, but at least they have gained experience in policy making by observing a complete policy analysis.

Without question the kinds of research and analysis involved in this second general approach to policy participation by economists-turned-social-scientists are difficult. It is fashionable in some quarters to say that effective work along these lines is impossible. It is argued first of all that the approach is too broad and demanding to be thorough — that a man cannot be an effective social scientist. Second, it is argued that all objectivity is lost when this approach is used, that the analysis becomes lost in a sea of unknown values — those of the analyst and those of society.

The above arguments cannot be disproved, but neither can they be proved. This much can be said, however, for the benefit of those persons who are generally sympathetic to the arguments developed in this chapter. It is easy to overemphasize the diversity of method among the social disciplines: statistics and logic acquired in one social discipline can be used without too much modification in the other disciplines. What is really required by this second approach is the breadth of training and the imagination to lead the social scientist into those fields where the consequences of a course of action are really important, and the willingness to inquire into the consequences involved in those different fields. It is also evident, or it should be, that one lone social scientist could not be expected to undertake all the various kinds of analyses suggested under this second approach to policy participation. It is enough to hope that a few economists and professional men from other disciplines might metamorphose into social scientists and attempt to deal, as time and training permit, with one or more of the phases outlined under this second approach.

126

This metamorphosis should not prove too difficult for some agricultural economists. Agricultural economists are in fact the social scientists of agriculture.[12] They are treated as such by farm people, and often behave as such before farm people. It is before their colleagues that they become cautious — careful to act like economists and talk like economists. What is recommended here, then, is that more agricultural economists openly and unashamedly attempt to play the role of social scientists. In so doing, they will become better trained and more effective social scientists, and some may drop the rather immature delineation of all social activity into economic and political. In so doing, they may come to recognize the equity implications of a course of action as well as the efficiency implications, the family and community implications as well as the output implications, the nonmoney costs as well as the money costs of human resource mobility, the recreational aspects of land use as well as the productive aspects, the aesthetic aspects of the landscape as well as its income-producing aspects, and so on. In other words, it is argued here that those agricultural economists who declare to themselves and to the public that they are acting as social scientists in the complexities of policy making will play a more effective role in that policy making than those who think they are economists but behave as if they were social scientists.

The question of the objectivity, or lack of objectivity of the second approach to policy participation needs to be considered too. It is difficult to see how less objectivity (or more value judgments) is involved in describing the consequences of a particular course of action in all the different fields of human activity, than in describing the economic consequences of alternative courses of action. The former task involves broader vistas than the second, but the problem of the investigator's values would seem the same in both instances. An analysis of the value systems of society may also be conducted with reasonable objectivity insofar as society permits analytical objectivity. The problem here is not so much that the investigator has personal biases as the fact that many social groups do not want their basic values examined and are intolerant of such analyses when made.

[12] A few rural sociologists (e.g., Carl C. Taylor and Lowry Nelson) have probably more nearly approached the goal of being general social scientists than any agricultural economist that might be named. But the fact is that the agricultural economists have the money, the attention of the public, and the numbers. Overwhelmingly they are the social scientists in agriculture.

Questions about values and the value judgments of the investigator do, however, come to the fore with respect to an appraisal of the various consequences of, and the drawing of conclusions with respect to the desirability of, a particular course of action. The question here is whether a complete analysis involving all facets of a policy problem, but necessarily incorporating the valuations of the investigator, is useful to policy decision-makers. Society must think so, for it clamors for and is deluged by the opinions of men and organizations on most policy issues. And this writer believes that a complete analysis by a social scientist of an important policy issue can be highly useful to lay decision-makers. This is true even when the conclusions run counter to lay thinking, for such an analysis will suggest what a complete analysis consists of; it will provide different analytical views of an old problem and hence it will serve to stimulate further thinking about the issues confronting decision-makers.

Moreover, if the value system of the investigator is well known or if he provides a portrait of his value system, consumers of the policy appraisal have a basis for converting or translating the investigator's conclusions into conclusions of their own. In other words, if the reader knows the scale of values that was used to appraise a particular course of action, he knows better how to evaluate the conclusions of the appraiser. Thus, less self-restraint and more discussion by policy analysts of their own value systems might lead to more illuminating and more useful policy appraisals.

The need for making explicit the value systems of social scientists dealing with explosive policy problems is stated clearly and beautifully by Myrdal:

Biases in research are much deeper seated than in the formulation of avowedly practical conclusions. They are not valuations *attached* to research but rather they *permeate* research. They are the unfortunate results of *concealed* valuations that insinuate themselves into research in all stages, from its planning to its final presentation.

The valuations will, when driven underground, hinder observation and inference from becoming truly objective. This can be avoided only by making the valuations explicit. *There is no other device for excluding biases in social sciences than to face the valuations and to introduce them as explicitly stated, specific, and sufficiently concretized value premises. . . .*[13]

[13] Myrdal, *op. cit.*, p. 1043.

The Values and Preconceptions of the Author

Because I will analyze and appraise certain agricultural price and income policies in Chapters 7 and 8, and because, further, it has been argued here that one way of dealing with the valuation problem in policy participation is to put the value systems of the principals out on the table for all to see, I shall in this section present a portrait of my system of values.

There are certain dangers in this procedure. First, it is open to misinterpretation: some people may view it as an egocentric, tasteless act. Second, and more important, the development of an accurate, representative portrait of one's own value system is difficult and perhaps impossible. One discovers that his values exist in different, noncomparable planes, that his values and beliefs [14] are inextricably intermixed, and that he is under pressure to present to the world a rational, internally consistent system of values. Myrdal was digging deep when he said:

. . . we . . . observe that the valuations simply cannot be treated as if they existed on the same plane. They refer to different levels of the moral personality . . . Some valuations concern human beings in general; others concern Negroes or women or foreigners; still others concern a particular group of Negroes or an individual Negro. Some valuations have general and eternal validity; others have validity only for certain situations.[15]

He continues:

. . . When the valuations are conflicting, as they normally are, beliefs serve the rationalization function of bridging illogicalities. The beliefs are thus not only determined by available scientific knowledge in society and the efficacy of the means of its communication to various population groups but are regularly "biased," by which we mean that they are systematically twisted in the one direction which fits them best for purposes of rationalization.[16]

But I will do my best to present an accurate and representative picture; that is all I can do.

The foremost, the paramount value in my system of values is the Golden Rule — thou shalt do unto others as you would have them do unto you. On this rock all my ethical values rest, and on this rock my

[14] Following Myrdal, ideas concerned with how reality is, or was, are here called beliefs. Ideas concerned with the worthwhileness of things, how they ought to be or ought not to be, are here called values.
[15] Myrdal, *op. cit.*, p. 1027.
[16] *Ibid.*, p. 1030.

personal behavior, I would argue, should rest. On this foundation value I build, and logically it seems to me, a philosophy of mutual responsibility: a belief that I am responsible in part for my neighbor's well-being and he for mine; a belief that a sympathetic consideration of the other fellow's position is indispensable to the good life widely shared in an interdependent society.

In the world of narrowly oriented efforts to earn a living, petty rivalries, and power struggles, this philosophy converts into an intense sympathy for the underdog. And in a society dominated, on the surface at least, by an ideology of individualism, this philosophy and this sympathy for the underdog translate into political action concerned with reform. Social situations, social forms, and institutions that permit, or contribute to, the domination of one man or one group by another man or group need to be changed — reformed. Thus, as I see it, the pre-eminent position of the Golden Rule in my system of values leads me to emphasize equity problems and to be vitally concerned with individual or group action designed to correct inequitable situations.

Consequently I highly prize efforts by individuals, by voluntary associations such as churches, and by government to redress inequitable situations. The efforts, for example, of private parties and institutions to provide scholarship to deserving scholars, the efforts of church groups to bring an end to the segregation of races, and the efforts of government to provide economic groups in weak bargaining positions with increased bargaining power are all to be commended and encouraged.

There is no suggestion in the foregoing that many people, in fact most people, do not value the Golden Rule positively. The question is, On what plane does this value exist for many people, or most people? Is it a secondary value, or a paramount value? I would argue that the evolutionary principle of "survival of the fittest" as given ethical content — fierce and fanatical ethical content — in the writings of Herbert Spencer and William Graham Sumner, and the commonplace ethical principle of "the Lord helps those that help themselves" are both in conflict with the Golden Rule. Persons who value either of the latter two ethical principles on the same plane with the ethic of the Golden Rule must either have developed an ingenious philosophical scheme of rationalization, or find it difficult to decide what is good behavior and what is bad. Those persons who place either of the latter two ethics at the top of their system of values must, if they reason logically as Spencer and Sumner did, accept a philosophy of rigorous individualism with its laissez-faire implications and overtones.

Another positive value of mine, but one far down the scale from the Golden Rule, is a high and rising material level of living for myself and others (i.e., the maximum output, and an increasing output per unit of input). But here an important preconception concerning the facts enters the picture. I *believe* that the dramatic output achievements of the Western world in general, and the United States in particular, have come about through research, development, and the adoption of new technologies, whereas economic theory emphasizes, almost to the exclusion of technological advance, the realization of an optimum allocation of productive resources. We can have, and have had, tremendous increases in output per unit of input in the United States through widespread technological advance, *but with some obviously poor allocations of human resources*. But the converse is not possible. Thus, the question arises: Why the preoccupation of economists with the static theory of resource allocation?

Like all people who take pride in our country I value certain of our institutions highly: our public school system, our Bill of Rights sullied as it may be from time to time by overzealous patriots, our near-universal suffrage, and our national forest and park system. All of these, and many others that could be named, give the United States a distinctive flavor; make it, I believe, a good place to live in. But there is one institution I value particularly, one that is currently undergoing rapid change and may be in danger, like the whooping crane, of passing out of existence. It is the family farm — the family farm as it flourished from the Alleghenys to the High Plains and north of the Ohio River. It once provided a way of life as well as a way of business, and to me it provided a good way of life. Now it provides primarily a way of business, and in years to come it may not provide even that in an owner-operator sense. With capital requirements running as high as $100,000 per farm it is difficult to see how these farms can remain family affairs. But what I want to say here is that I think our country will be losing something vital if it loses the institution of the owner-operated family farm.

As far as I know, I am indifferent to the question of government ownership and operation of productive resources. In some cases (e.g., the Rural Electrification Administration) government ownership seems to work wonderfully well; in others, where negotiation and transactions

131

take many and varied forms, it seems to lead to inefficiencies and personal corruption. Thus, I do not hold government ownership to be either good or bad; I want to look at the merits of each individual case.

There are, however, some things that I don't like — some things that I value negatively. They are:

1. A more unequal distribution of income than we currently have in the United States.

2. A more rapid rate of technological advance in both the farm and nonfarm sectors than we now have, with the social adjustment and institutional changes that a more rapid rate of technological advance would entail.

3. An ideology and policies designed to move in the direction of an intense individualism on one hand, or the corporate state on the other.

Many more items, some large and many small, are included in my system of values. And each of the above items could be elaborated upon at great length. But they will not be, for the above incomplete list makes clear in a general sense what I hold to be of value to society, and what I don't. It describes in a rough way the system of values that I cannot escape bringing to bear on any appraisal of policy. These are my value premises; these values I cannot escape using in judging and appraising alternative courses of action.

I can see certain inconsistencies — valuation conflicts — that show up around the edges of the above picture. There are no doubt others. A high and increasing material level of living is important to me; I prize the good life as measured in material terms. But I don't want a too rapid rate of technological advance, and I deprecate the present emphasis on gadgets and power tools. I hanker for the old days with respect to certain institutions — for the family farm as it existed before World War I, and for the tight family groups that existed before transportation became so accessible and cheap. On the other hand, I value highly social and political reforms designed to weed out and alleviate inequitable situations. There are valuation conflicts here, but most of the time they do not cause me serious trouble. Most of the time I successfully keep these conflicting values in their respective pigeonholes.

No item listed above can be *proved* to be of positive value, or of negative value, to society. These values do not lend themselves to that kind of treatment. Each can be demonstrated to be good or bad only in terms of some other value. But these are things that I *judge* to be worthwhile to some degree to someone. If a man's values are too different from those of his fellow men he can, however, get into trouble. For example, a few men in the United States want more than one wife; they value polygamy highly. Society takes a different view of polygamy: valuing monogamous marriages highly, it says that polygamy is bad, and a man caught practicing polygamy is sent to jail. But polygamy has not been *proven* wrong: it has been *judged* wrong in terms of the cultural unity existing within the United States.

Last, but not least, it should be recognized that the portrait of my value system has been presented as if it were a static thing, but it is not. I know that it has changed over the years, and I expect it to continue to change in future years (at least I hope so, although this hope is itself a value, a prizing). My value system — the objects, acts, and ideas cherished or valued by me in varying degrees — will certainly undergo continuous reconstruction if my field of possible conduct or action continues to widen. In other words, what I prize and to what degree I prize it, will depend upon what it is possible for me to do and to participate in doing. And my field of possible conduct may be expected to widen through personal experiences in social action, through personal inquiry and research, and, most important, through the researches and inquiries of scholars everywhere.

7

The Blind Policy Alleys

THE time has come to talk policy. And we will begin this discussion by looking at some of the blind alleys of agricultural price and income policy in the United States. In other words, we will begin by sweeping away some of the fantasy and folklore concerning agricultural price and income policy and pointing out those courses of action that lead down blind alleys.

As used here, what does the phrase "the blind alleys of agricultural price and income policy" mean? We will have in mind here two possibilities: (1) a course of action that is incapable of achieving its stated objective(s); and (2) a course of action that gives rises to new problems — situations which the persons involved, as well as other members of society, consider intolerable and seek to avoid. A policy approach that fits into either of these two categories is a blind alley approach.

There are a lot of these dead-end approaches around. Most farmers, as well as many agricultural economists, have one or more that they are willing to trot out for inspection and discussion on the slightest provocation. Further, there are many combinations of the more widely known approaches. The discussion in this chapter will, however, be limited to the more widely known or discussed approaches. Each will be discussed in its most commonly accepted form and as an isolated approach. The implications of various combinations of these policy approaches must be inferred by the reader, but this should not be too difficult.

The Free Market Approach
Relatively speaking, there are not many people who advocate a return to the free market for agriculture. A few farmers do; of these a still fewer

number could, because of their aggressiveness and strong asset positions, weather the price-income storm that would follow. Most farmer advocates of a return to the free market have little or no conception of the price-income consequences of such a course of action. The advocates of a return to the free market for agriculture are relatively more numerous among city dwellers. Spokesmen for big and little business, as well as many economists, tend to gather in this camp. But most farmers, and city people as well, feel that farmers need the help of government in these troublesome 1950s, and will continue to need it from time to time in the future. In other words, most laymen share the second variant of the myth as given content by the Committee for the Twentieth Century Fund (see pp. 5–7).

There is some question as to what is meant by a return to a free market. How quickly is this return to take place, and if it should, what would happen to government-held stocks of agricultural commodities? Does getting government out of agriculture also mean the elimination of governmental support for research and development work, the Extension Service, the Soil Conservation Service, the Market News Service, and so on? Advocates of a free market generally do not find the provision of the latter services by government undesirable; either implicitly or explicitly they recognize that these services are prerequisites to an expanding food supply. But those who favor a return to the free market generally feel that the free market should not be burdened by government stocks accumulated under a price-supported market.

So in this analysis of the workings of a free market for agriculture, we shall assume the somewhat inconsistent position held by exponents of that policy persuasion, namely: (1) stocks accumulated by government under past price supporting operations are abolished — burned, buried, or given away; (2) most research and service work in agriculture will be continued; and (3) all price and income supporting operations are eliminated. This, it will be recognized, is a "free market mechanism" where the engine of technological advance is left running, but the engine of price and income support has been shut off.

If the volume of agricultural surplus in the middle 1950s is running at the annual rate of 4 to 5 per cent, as is generally conceded, then to clear these surplus stocks through the free market, the level of farm prices would have to fall by 50 to 60 per cent. This conclusion follows from the workings of the aggregative model presented in Chapter 3.

There can be no question about it: a return to the free market in the 1950s would precipitate a major price level decline in agriculture.

But if farm prices were permitted to fall on the average by 50 to 60 per cent from the 1956–57 level and then were left entirely alone, this drastic action would *in time* correct the surplus condition and start prices moving up once again. These very low farm prices and the financial losses that they would entail, would first wipe out the liquid assets of most farmers; second, in time they would also wear away and destroy the fixed assets of most farmers (a few of the most efficient and well-financed farmers might expand during the bad years and prosper with rising prices when they came). As the asset positions of farmers worsened and turned increasingly into liabilities, the ability of farmers to adopt new capital-using technologies and to replace worn out capital items would be restricted and then shut off. In this way, the rate of aggregate output expansion would be slowed down and brought into equality with the rate of aggregate demand expansion. So in time — perhaps five years, perhaps ten or fifteen years — the farm price level would move upward again as aggregate demand pushed ahead of aggregate supply.

This is what is known as putting agriculture through the long-run wringer. Through widespread financial losses and business failure, the rate of farm technological advance and capital formation is slowed down, and with it the rate of aggregate output expansion. The long-run wringer "corrects" the surplus condition that originated the price decline, and *in time* starts farm prices moving upward again.

It is also assumed by those who favor such a free market that low farm prices would speed up the flow of labor out of agriculture, and thus act to reduce total resource inputs. This assumption is a questionable one. The flow of human resources out of agriculture is probably more closely associated with nonfarm job opportunities than with changes in the level of farm product prices relative to the level of nonfarm prices. Further, extreme agricultural poverty may act to starve farm people into agriculture rather than out. Falling farm prices *may* act to reduce labor inputs in agriculture, depending upon circumstances on the nonfarm side of the fence, but the supply-reducing effects of this approach are guaranteed from another source. They are guaranteed by the failure to replace capital items and the failure to adopt new capital-using technologies where financial losses are widespread. Capital starvation, not human starvation, ensures a slowdown in the rate of aggregate output expansion through the workings of the long-run wringer.

This ability of the free market approach to reduce surpluses is the seductive feature of this approach for economic logicians and others not themselves affected by changes in such markets (e.g., publishers of newspapers enjoying local monopolies, chairmen of boards of directors of corporations producing differentiated and hence monopolistic products). The beauty of it is that by doing nothing the wringer operates to correct the surplus condition in the *long run*. But the long-run wringer of widespread financial losses and business failure runs headlong into the democratic ethic of reasonably fair incomes for everyone.

Most people in the United States *value* highly good and stable incomes for themselves and their friends and neighbors. True, they may not want their friends and neighbors to get ahead of them or even quite come up to them, incomewise; but they do value or prize a fair return for a job fairly done. And they *believe* that such incomes on a continuing basis are dependent upon the receipt of reasonably good and stable incomes by everyone else (i.e., one sector of the economy cannot be prosperous unless the other sectors are). This *value* and this *belief* convert into the democratic ethic, or basis of behavior and action, of fair incomes for everyone.

Most Americans no longer believe that general business depressions should be "cured" through the free market corrective process, or that major segments of the economy should be forced through that "natural" process. They believe that persons who work hard in generally recognized industries, trades, and professions are entitled to fair incomes. (Besides, it might be dangerous to let the incomes of a major segment of the economy sag; we might all get sucked into the downward spiral.) Thus, beautiful as the long-run, free-market corrective process may be on paper, it runs into violent opposition among real people. Real, live people with hopes and aspirations for themselves, family, and friends do not want to correct imbalances in the economy by means of widespread financial losses and business failure. Real, live people want to find more humane methods than the free market to correct inequitable situations and maladjustments in the economy. And they do not hesitate to make government an instrument of such humane methods.

Thus, the free market approach turns out to be a blind alley approach. Given sufficient time, it can slow down the rate of aggregate output expansion and even reduce aggregate output in agriculture. But it gives rise to other problems, income problems, that society wants to avoid. Given the dominant values and beliefs of present-day society, a responsible government cannot pursue a free market course of action in agriculture.

The Flexible Price Support Approach

The flexible price support approach is a first cousin to the free market approach. Proponents of flexible price supports see in this approach the opportunity to get the good (i.e., supply-reducing aspects) of the free market without the bad (i.e., the severe income declines). This can be accomplished, they argue, by lowering the price of one commodity relative to the prices of other commodities as stocks of the first commodity accumulate in the hands of the government. Although the law has never made changes in the level of price support for a commodity mandatory, the approach assumes that the level of price support for a commodity will vary inversely with the excess supply of the commodity. The assumption made here is that the production of this commodity will decline as the supported price of it falls relative to other commodity prices.

A brief summary of the flexible price provision of the Agricultural Act of 1954 is given below:

Mandatory price support at 90 per cent of parity now in effect for the six basic commodities — wheat, corn, cotton, rice, tobacco, and peanuts — will be allowed to expire with the 1954 crops, and flexible price supports, ranging from 75 per cent to 90 per cent of parity according to supply conditions, will go into effect, except that for the 1955 crops, the minimum level of price support for the basic commodities willl be 82½ per cent of parity. The Act does not affect the level at which tobacco is required to be supported. Under existing law, which is not affected, tobacco is required to be supported at 90 per cent of parity if marketing quotas are in effect.[1]

It is also the case that the level of price support on the "basic" commodities was held close to 80 per cent of parity through 1956 and 1957, and that the level of price support on manufactured dairy products was raised to above 80 per cent in 1956.

The optimism of proponents of the flexible price support approach with regard to its supply-reducing potential grows out of the old fallacy

---

[1] *Summary of the Agricultural Act of 1954*, prepared by the Office of the Solicitor of the U.S. Department of Agriculture.

of composition.[2] With a decline in the price of a commodity, say, hogs, these folks observe that farmers start cutting back the supply of hogs by shifting resources out of the production of hogs and into commodity substitutes. Farmers' responses are similar for such commodities as eggs, potatoes, cotton, soy beans, cabbage, and any other commodity with close production substitutes. If the price of one commodity falls relative to other commodities, and if farmers can shift out of it, *they will.*

But the aggregate is a different story. The substitutional possibilities open to the farm firm are completely different from those of a single enterprise on the farm. When all farm commodity prices are falling, there is no place for the farmer to hide. It does not help to shift resources among farm enterprises and the farmer cannot readily shift his productive resources into the production of such things as soap, T.V. sets, or fishing poles. Hence, the representative farmer employs his resources fully where he can, namely in farming, and continues to turn out as much total product from his farm as he can; this means that all farm commodity prices can fall a long, long way and remain low for a long, long time without inducing a contraction in aggregate output.

Reasoning from a commodity part to the agricultural whole thus leads protagonists of flexible price supports astray. Available evidence indicates this to be the case at present. Between 1951 and 1956 the index of prices received for all farm commodities declined 22 per cent, as total farm output increased by almost 13 per cent. True, all of this price decline did not result from a reduction in the level of price supports; a large share of it resulted from the falling down of commodity prices to support levels. But a price level decline is a price level decline whether it results from prices falling in an unsupported market, or in a supported market. A price level decline of 22 per cent did not slow up the rate of aggregate output expansion in the early 1950s, let alone decrease aggregate output.

In this connection, it is incorrect to picture the total economy as a large static operation in which relative price changes between segments of the economy transfer resources at will between these segments. The total economy is a growing, developing thing with labor moving toward the skilled and service trades and capital moving into processing, fabrication, and agriculture. In this context of growth, the critical adjustment for agriculture is the adjustment of the rate of output expansion to the

[2] See the discussion of this concept in the introduction to Chapter 3, p. 34.

rate of demand expansion. And this the falling farm price level between 1951 and 1956 did not begin to accomplish.

Next it should be recognized that the Republican administration lowered the level of price support on commodities coming under support from only 90 per cent of parity to something close to 80 per cent of parity between 1954 and 1957. Flexible price supports became inflexible in the neighborhood of 80 per cent of parity, even though the government continued to accumulate surplus stocks of agricultural commodities. The reason that the level of flexible price support stiffened, and stuck at or near 80 per cent of parity is that this general approach ran into the solidly held democratic ethic of reasonably fair incomes for everyone at that level of farm prices. Politicians who earn their livings by gauging and reflecting the values and beliefs of society reached the conclusion that society did not want farm prices to fall further; these politicians reached the conclusion that they could not live through the social and economic unrest that would result from lowering the level of farm price support below 80 per cent of parity. The Republican administration, in lowering price support levels to the neighborhood of 80 per cent of parity, reached the lower limits of political tolerance with respect to farm prices, given the values and beliefs of society in the 1950s.[3]

But lowering price support levels a few percentage points did not, and will not, get the government out of the price-supporting business. No one knows how low farm prices would have to go and how long they would have to stay there in order to first slow down the rate of aggregate output expansion and then contract aggregate output; but those prices would have to fall a long way and stay there a long time to bring aggregate output back into line with demand. They would have to fall much farther than politicians, reflecting the hopes and aspirations of farm people and other people as well, are going to let them fall.

The flexible price support approach turns out to be a blind alley sealed off at both ends. At a level of price support of 80 to 82 per cent of parity, aggregate output gives promise of outracing aggregate demand into the indefinite future. By this approach incomes are not

---

[3] This, of course, does not mean that various people or organizations will not try to reduce levels of price support below 80 per cent of parity. In the spring of 1957 Secretary Benson suggested once again that price support levels be lowered, with the implication that they should be lowered drastically. Whether he will win approval for such a policy from leaders of his own political party and against the opposition of the Democratic party is, however, another question.

reduced sufficiently to choke off the rate of farm technological advance via the farm asset nexus. But this approach gives no promise of improving farm incomes in the foreseeable future. This approach, like the free market approach, is impaled on the twin horns of the surplus problem and the income problem. To correct one problem through "natural" processes, the second problem must be intensified beyond a point acceptable to society. Thus, neither problem is resolved.

In Chapter 2, it will be recalled, two problems — an income problem and an uncertainty problem — were outlined. The income problem resulted from price level instability, and the uncertainty problem from commodity price variability around the moving farm price level. The flexible price support approach under discussion here has the capacity to deal with the uncertainty problem (i.e., to take the uncertainty out of individual commodity prices in the forthcoming production period), but it lacks the capacity to deal with the income problem. It cannot reduce aggregate output and restore farm prices and incomes to satisfactory levels without first letting farm prices and incomes fall to levels unacceptable to society. We have in flexible price supports an example of an approach designed to deal with one kind of problem (the commodity price uncertainty problem) being employed to deal with another kind of problem (the general income problem in commercial agriculture) for which it was not designed. It has failed to do what it was not designed to do, namely, correct the general income problem in commercial agriculture.

The Farm Efficiency Approach

The farm efficiency approach is essentially the business analyst's or farm manager's approach to the price-income problems of commercial agriculture. Farm managers have observed that the very efficient farmers who entered the period 1951–56 in a strong financial position have done rather well during this period. The labor-management incomes of such farmers have not declined as much as those of average farmers, and in some cases they have been increasing. Further, these are the fellows who in the 1950s are expanding the size of their farms and are becoming large-scale, commercial operators. Proponents of this approach reason that if all farms were large-scale and highly efficient, labor-management incomes to the owner-operators would be high, or at least not declining, and the chronic price-income problem in agriculture would be solved.

141

This approach is generally associated in some way with one or the other of the two previous approaches. The emphasis, however, is clearly different. Proponents of the free market and the flexible price support approaches tacitly assume that agriculture would develop into a set of financially strong, large-scale, efficient, commercial farms under either of those approaches. But price is the motivating factor of those approaches. Proponents of the make-all-farms-efficient approach, on the other hand, tacitly assume the workings of a free market and stress good business management as the means of achieving a set of financially strong, large-scale, efficient, commercial farms. These folks see research and education in business management as the key motivating factor.

We should be clear, also, that advocates of this approach do not visualize making each of the nearly three million commercial farms, as of 1954, into a financially strong, large-scale, efficient farm. This approach is dependent upon a high rate of mobility out of agriculture. It assumes that the great exodus of human resources off the land that began in the late 1930s will continue, and that the land and other resources formerly operated by the people who have moved to town will be incorporated into the remaining farms. In this way the size of the remaining farms is increased. In this view — given the state of the arts in the middle 1950s — perhaps one and a half million commercial farms would be an optimum number rather than three million. In any event, proponents of this approach foresee many fewer farms, much larger farms, and much more efficient farms.

What are the characteristics of these financially strong, large-scale, efficient, commercial farms? The key characteristics are high yields per acre, high yields per animal, high capital investment, and high worker productivity. In other words, these farms are efficient *because output per bundle of resources employed is high.* These farms are paying a reasonable return to capital and a satisfactory labor-management return because they produce more product for sale per bundle of resources employed than do average, or representative, farms. Large and expanding output per unit of input, measured in value terms, is the not-so-secret key to success on these farms.

Bearing these considerations in mind, what if the agriculture of the United States were transformed overnight, or within a few short years, into one and a half million large-scale, highly efficient, commercial farms all employing the best production practices in the best business organizations? *What if?* The answer is obvious. The nightmare that average and laggard farmers have been living through in the 1950s would envelop the highly efficient farmers on their broad and productive acres. If the best production practices in the best business organizations were generally employed throughout agriculture, rather than on the relatively few large-scale, highly efficient farms, farm commodities would be running out the ears of every consumer, *unless total inputs employed in agriculture, not just labor inputs, were drastically reduced.* Given the highly inelastic demand for food, farm commodity prices would likely be on the minus side of zero. Moving to a highly efficient agriculture across the board within a few years would shoot aggregate supply past aggregate demand and precipitate a farm price level decline that is not pleasant to contemplate.

Proponents of this approach too have fallen into the trap of the fallacy of composition. Because some relatively efficient farmers can and do make reasonably good labor-management returns under a price level that squeezes the representative farmer, it does not follow that the way to cure the ills of agriculture is to make every farmer as efficient as the most efficient. Making every farmer as efficient as the most efficient changes the situation under which the most efficient were prospering; it changes the situation by increasing aggregate output importantly and decreasing the farm price level importantly. Since the aggregate demand for farm food products is very inelastic, gross returns to the aggregate of efficient farmers must fall sharply. In the new and drastically reduced price level situation where every farmer is a highly efficient farmer, those farmers too would feel a cost-price squeeze.

Some evidence can be adduced in support of the above argument. In 1952 a joint Land Grant College Department of Agriculture Committee on Agriculture's Capacity to Produce issued the following statement with regard to attainable increases in output over the period 1951–55:

Despite the high levels of recent years, farm production could be expanded still further. . . . The volume of output attainable by 1955 would be about 20 percent greater than in 1950 and 18 percent above the outturn of 1951. . . .

Of prime importance in a defense setting is the estimate that a one-fifth increase in farm output could be obtained with about the same acreage of farm land and man-hours of farm labor as in 1951. Higher production per acre, per animal unit, and per man-hour of farm labor would keynote the record output that would be attainable by 1955.

Fertilizer, machinery, and other production goods, all of which are necessary for an expanded use of improved crop and livestock practices, would continue to be substituted for both farm land and farm labor in reaching the level of output attainable by 1955.

The use of about 70 percent more fertilizer than in 1950 would contribute importantly to a 17-percent rise in crop production per acre. Moreover, the increase in crop yields would be obtained in a pattern of cropland use that would represent progress in soil conservation. The proportion of cropland in intertilled crops would increase slightly above that of 1950 but it would be less than in 1951. The proportion in sod crops and close-growing crops would increase.

Greater production of feed crops and pasture would make possible a 13-percent increase in the number of animal units of breeding livestock, while improved feeding and other production practices would raise output per breeding unit 6 percent above the 1950 level.[4]

The above estimate of an 18 per cent increase in total farm output over the period of 1951–55 was not set up as a distant, unrealistic target. It describes the increase in total output attainable within a four-year period where farmers generally made effective use of *known* technologies — became reasonably efficient in terms of the state of the arts in 1951. It was made as a first approximation of what was attainable over the period 1951–55 with the basic farm organizational structure of 1951, and taking into consideration what would be profitable to farmers given the price-cost structure of 1951.

Actually, total farm output did not increase by 18 per cent over the period 1951–55 for at least two reasons: (1) the patriotic motive was lost with the ending of the Korean "police action" and (2) the farm price level fell substantially during the period. Total farm output did, however, increase by 9 or 10 per cent over the period in question (depending on the index of output used); this increase in total farm output, given the increase in demand and the price support structure, caused the farm price level to decline some 22 per cent. In a free market situation the price level decline would have been in the neighborhood of 50 per cent (see the analysis of the working model in Chapter 3, pp. 56–57).

Suppose now that total farm output had increased by 18 per cent between 1951 and 1955. In this unlikely event — assumed here because in a sense it was attainable — the surplus stocks accumulated by government would have had to increase from 4 to 6 per cent of the total supply

[4] *Agriculture's Capacity to Produce*, U.S.D.A., Agr. Info. Bul. No. 88, June 1952, pp. 4–5.

to 12 to 15 per cent of the total supply under price supports, or the farm price level would have had to fall to, or near, zero in a free market situation. The fact that neither of the above developments would have occurred in the world of reality is irrelevant to this discussion. The increase in output that could induce these developments was, in fact, attainable where *all farms* made some realistic gains in efficiency over a four-year period. Such an increase in output over a four-year period in the 1950s would have been sufficient to wreck either the government price support program or the price level.

What then would have happened in the way of an output-increasing action between 1951 and 1955 if the structure of agriculture had been changed by the emergence of one and a half million large-scale, highly efficient farms, and the price level had fallen some 22 per cent — which it did? Since we cannot rerun the course of history to find out, no one will ever know for sure. But it seems evident to this writer that total output would have increased by at least the 18 per cent estimated by the joint committee, and perhaps a great deal more. In other words, getting rid of the average farmer and the laggards and making every farm operation as efficient as the most efficient would have offset, or more than offset, the negative effects on production of a price level decline of 22 per cent. If this view is correct, the increase in total output over the period 1951–55, resulting from the conversion of agriculture into a set of large-scale, highly efficient farm operations, would either have completely wrecked the price support programs of the period, or wrecked the price level itself.

The saving grace in all this is, of course, that the structure of agriculture cannot be changed within a few years to one where each farm is financially strong, large-scale, and as efficient as the most efficient. Numerous restrictions make such a goal impossible of attainment: the rate of capital formation, the rate of information dissemination and knowledge absorption, the rate of migration off farms, and the perversity of human beings. But the important point to keep in mind is that the pursuit of a course of action designed to speed up the making of all farms efficient in the context of the 1950s and 1960s must act to speed up the rate of aggregate output expansion, and hence contribute to a further decline in the farm price level as well as to a further decline in aggregate gross income.

This conclusion raises a fundamental question. Are we to conclude that the goal of increased efficiency, which is highly valued by most members of society inside agriculture and out, is undesirable? The answer to this question is *no* in the sense in which greater efficiency is generally prized — namely, as helping to provide a rising real level of living in the growing, developing economy. But the answer is *yes* in the sense of providing a solution to the price-income problems of commercial agriculture in the 1950s.

In a growing, developing economy, increased efficiency growing out of farm technological advance permits labor employed in agriculture to be released and to be re-employed in enterprises producing products and services with high income elasticities — the manufacture and sale of automobiles, teaching, medical services, entertainment). This is what economic progress means; transferring human labor from food-producing industries to service-providing industries is a necessary part of economic progress. But the development of greater efficiency in agriculture must bear some relation to the total growth process; it must take place as an integral part, not as an independent part, of the growing economy; it must release men for nonfarm employment and provide a food supply for the growing population in accordance with the needs of the developing economy.

The development of a crash program in agriculture to make each farm operation as efficient as the most efficient, *as a means of dealing with the price-income problems of commercial agriculture,* can only lead to greater problems. Greatly enhanced efficiency across the board in agriculture must speed up the rate of aggregate output expansion, and thus further increase the pressure of food supplies on population. The goal of greater efficiency and a course of action aimed at that goal, which is highly desirable for the individual farmer in the context of average farmers, and for total society in the context of a growing, developing economy, turns out to be a blind alley for dealing with the price-income problems of commercial agriculture in the 1950s.

The Fixed Price Support Approach

The fixed price support approach is the best known of the various approaches to the price-income problems of commercial agriculture. It traces its lineage back to the price-supporting programs of the 1930s, but in its modern form it was developed during World War II to protect farmers against an expected postwar slump. Gradually, however, the fixed price support approach became *the* price policy of the Democratic party, and was employed extensively through 1954, when it gave way to the policy of flexible price supports.

The fixed price support idea is the ultimate in simplicity. A fair, or reasonable, price to farmers is defined by Congress and maintained in the marketplace through government action. The government guarantees to support the prices of certain commodities (in practice the so-called "basics"[5] and other politically important commodities such as dairy products) in the market at some percentage of parity (in practice the level of price support has generally been fixed at 90 per cent of parity, but it could be higher or lower). Price support in the market is achieved thus: an agency of the federal government acquires and removes supplies from the market by means of direct purchases and non-recourse loans; the stocks so acquired are then stored by the government in the expectation or hope that they may be distributed outside the commercial channels of trade. In any event, the government cannot pour its stocks back onto the market unless prices rise, for some such reason as war, above the support level.

Production controls of any form or intensity could be linked to this approach, but in practice such controls have been considered secondary. They have been applied commodity by commodity, as the stocks of a commodity held by government became burdensome. The resources employed in the production of the commodity or commodities currently in surplus shifted into the production of other commodities — typically non-price-supported commodities. Production controls never really controlled production (i.e., reduced total output) under this approach; they simply shunted resources around a bit among commodities.

The approach we are considering, then, is the price support program of the Democratic administration of the early 1950s: fixed price supports at 90 per cent of parity, supply removal through purchases and non-recourse loans, and limited production controls. Farmers generally liked this approach. And why shouldn't they? It was a "heads I win, tails you lose" approach for them. Guaranteed prices at 90 per cent of parity do two important things: they remove or reduce year-to-year price uncertainty, and they protect the farmer against precipitous declines in gross income. In other words, this approach solves for the individual

[5] Cotton, corn, wheat, tobacco, peanuts, and rice.

147

farmer, at little or no cost, two critical problems confronting him — price uncertainty and ruinously low incomes.

In this favorable economic climate (it would be ideal from the viewpoint of farmers if the level of price support were somewhat higher) farmers react as any businessman might be expected to react. They invest in needed capital items, they adopt new technologies, *and they expand output.* They put into practice all those things that production experts have told them they should be doing, and thus increase their supply of marketable products for sale at a guaranteed price — a price which, if not exceptionally high, is not exceptionally low. In this favorable economic climate the means of financing new practices and technologies is not difficult to obtain. So the total situation acts to expand total output.

A policy of price support at 90 per cent of parity must, through its output-increasing effects, destroy itself in peacetime. In terms of operator family income, or incentive income, price support at 90 per cent of parity may not yield incomes comparable with nonfarm incomes. But it protects against income disaster, it protects established asset positions, and it reinforces the incentive to reduce unit costs — to reduce unit costs below an assured price. Thus, price supports at or near 90 per cent of parity become a mighty engine of farm output expansion, powering that expansion along at a rapid rate by means of the rapid and widespread adoption of new technologies.

Granted the output-expanding force of farm technological advance under good and guaranteed prices, the point to be made here is that the government could not maintain a policy of price support at 90 per cent of parity over any extended period with production and marketing controls no more effective than those developed in the past. The surplus stocks that would accumulate in government warehouses under guaranteed prices at 90 per cent of parity would wreck the program. Society will not tolerate the mismanagement and wastage of food supplies: witness the furor created by the killing of little pigs in the 1930s, the burning of potatoes in the 1940s, and the existence of large wheat stocks in the 1950s. The mountain of food stocks that would accumulate in government hands under this fixed price support approach would testify to gross mismanagement.

If people generally did not feel that it was wrong to waste or destroy food, or if food could be stored indefinitely in unlimited amounts and program costs were no consideration, then we could produce food in an irresponsible fashion to pour into bottomless storehouses, or into the ocean as in the case of the salt mill in the fairy tale "Why the Sea Is Salt." But cost is a consideration and the wasting of food is so generally and so intensely felt to be wrong (probably the result of the age-old pressure of population on food supplies) that no government could pursue a policy of storing or wasting all the food that farmers wanted to produce in the interests of maintaining farm incomes. People generally are not opposed to fair incomes for farmers, but they are opposed to producing food for storage bins. Costly and widespread storage operations that end in distribution scandals and destruction must give way before the deeply held value of conserving and husbanding food supplies.

Proponents of fixed price supports and limited production controls sometimes argue that the policy "worked" between 1932 and 1952. The policy did not "work"; it "lucked" through. Severe drought cut total output in the period 1934–36; World War II rescued the program in 1941 and 1942 as stocks were becoming unmanageable; and the Korean "affair" saved the program in 1950. Fortunately, no new war has come along since the Korean action to devour the government-owned stocks of agricultural commodities.

Proponents of this approach may then argue that it was fortunate for all concerned that the federal government had large stocks of agricultural commodities on hand at the outbreak of the two wars mentioned. And in this they are correct. So it may be argued persuasively that we should maintain large strategic food reserves as one part of our national security policy. But the highly productive agricultural plant of the United States could fill up any reasonable food reserve in a year or two. What then? There is no getting around one overwhelming fact — the agricultural plant of the United States can turn out more food and fiber products than the domestic population needs or can use in the foreseeable future with or without strategic food reserves.

It will be observed that the fixed price support approach is the exact converse of the free market approach. The free market approach solved the surplus problem in agriculture with no regard to the income problem of farmers. The fixed price support approach solves the income problem of farmers with no regard to the surplus problem. Each solves one problem by intensifying another. For this reason, each by itself is a blind policy alley.

149

The Domestic Food Consumption Approach

Interested laymen, social workers, farm leaders, and politicians have asked time and time again: Can't the food needs of the very poor and the moderately poor be linked to the chronic tendency for agriculture to overproduce, thereby eliminating or materially reducing, within the United States, the food problem on the one hand and the farm problem on the other. In other words, isn't our problem to find a way to turn the food needs of the very poor and the moderately poor into effective demand? And once the food needs of these folks have been converted into demand, won't the current surplus melt away like a snowball in July?

As we shall see, the answers to these questions fall on the negative side as far as the surplus problem is concerned, and hence as far as the price-income problems of commercial agriculture are concerned. But some words of caution or qualification should be interjected at this point. The increasing food consumption approach is most often suggested as a supplement to other approaches, and in this supplemental role it may merit serious consideration. Society may consider the objectives of safeguarding the diets of those living in poverty and the upgrading of the diets of low income people generally as important objectives, and wish to take collective action to realize those objectives without regard to the capacity, or lack of capacity, of this approach to solve the price-income problems of commercial agriculture. The discussion that follows is limited to the potentialities of the food consumption approach on the domestic scene.

THE FOOD CONSUMPTION SITUATION IN THE UNITED STATES

In brief, the facts of the food consumption picture in the United States are as follows: In 1955 there were some 3.3 million families and another 4.1 million single individuals with incomes of less than $1000 per year. In total there were nearly 15 million people living in or near poverty in 1955. According to the 1955 Household Food Consumption Survey, the caloric intake of most of these people in the lowest income class was adequate, but the diets of many of these people were deficient in important nutrients. The diets of over half the family members in this lowest income group were deficient in ascorbic acid, about one third were deficient in calcium, vitamin A, and riboflavin, and about one fourth were deficient in protein.

Technically, it would be possible for all the persons in this bottom income class to purchase and consume a nutritionally adequate diet composed of five commodities — wheat flour, lard, cheese, cabbage, and carrots. But Americans will not choose such a diet; it violates the common and generally accepted taste and preference patterns of our society, the strong preference of Americans for animal products, bakery products, and variety in the diet. What is important is the fact that the 15 million persons falling into this income class would find it next to impossible to purchase a nutritionally adequate diet consistent with the common and generally accepted taste and preference patterns of our society.

In 1955 there were about 15 million families, as well as an additional 4.5 million single individuals, with incomes between $1000 and $3999. Taking into account average family sizes, some 57 million people were living in this range of income. They typically do not suffer from an inadequate caloric intake (the converse is more likely to be the case), although there are many who suffer from an inadequate consumption of one or more nutrients. Nutritional deficiencies are, however, much less of a problem in the income group from $3000 to $3999 than in the lowest income group, $1000 and under. Moving from the lowest income class to the $3000 to $3999 income class, the percentage of people deficient in ascorbic acid declines from 51 to 26, in calcium from 37 to 31, in vitamin A from 36 to 18, in riboflavin from 32 to 17, and in protein from 23 to 6.

The exciting aspect of the food consumption pattern over the income range $500 to $3500 is not the incidence of nutritional deficiencies, which because of various food policies [6] are no longer serious on any wide scale, *but rather the important increases in expenditures for food that occur over that income range.* According to the 1955 Survey, family expenditures for food increased two and one third times between the lowest income level and the $3000 to $3999 level. These increased expenditures do not, however, go into more pounds; they go into increased food services and increased quantities of high-resource-using foods such as animal products and fruits and vegetables, as low-resource-using foods such as cereals are dropped out of the diet. To illustrate, the consumption of meat increased 50 per cent, of fresh fruits more than 50 per cent, and of canned and frozen fruits and vegetables and juices more

[6] Food enrichment programs, free milk and school lunches, and the dissemination of nutritional information.

than 50 per cent between the lowest income group and the $3000 to $3999 income group, while the consumption of flour and other cereal products declined 50 per cent.

Taking into account the spectacular changes in food consumption described above, as well as the lesser changes involved, the index of per capita food consumption increases by about 25 per cent as family incomes increase from the mean of $500 to $3500. In other words, the demand for food-producing resources, but not necessarily the same resources, by an average family increases by approximately 25 per cent as it moves from an average income of $500 to an average income of $3500. Further, and perhaps of greater importance, *purchases* of farm food products increase by 70 to 80 per cent as families move up the income ladder from an average of $500 to an average of $3500, since many of the poorest families produce much of their own food supply.

THE POLICY AVENUES

It has long been the policy of established welfare agencies at state and local levels to distribute food directly — by means of the food relief and charity programs — to very poor families and individuals. It has been the policy of the federal government during periods of farm surpluses to provide these agencies with surplus food items for distribution to needy families and individuals. This the federal government is doing and has been doing for several years. Also, some 11 million children, or roughly 30 per cent of the total number of children in grade and high schools, are participating in the National School Lunch Program as of 1957. Some 16 million children are now drinking milk under the school lunch and milk programs. Because these programs can help protect the health of one of the most vulnerable groups in society, and because they provide children with an experience in good eating (a live educational experience in good nutrition), these programs are highly valued on welfare grounds.

The above programs are the principal progeny of the marriage of nutrition research and farm surpluses in the United States. Each has developed into a sizable program, but each could be expanded. For example, no food policy exists and no food programs have been developed to meet the needs of the aged — the retired and the old folks that are simply waiting. This vulnerable group has been by-passed in this age of food opulence.

If the above programs were expanded to guarantee nutritionally adequate diets to those relatively few members of our national society who do not have such diets — primarily the 15 million persons falling in the lowest income group, but some others as well — total food consumption would be expanded somewhat, but probably not importantly. This is true for several reasons. First and foremost, the nutritionally adequate diet typically made available to the very poor and other vulnerable groups is a low-cost diet, composed of inexpensive, low-resource-using food items, rather than demand-expanding, high-resource-using food items. In other words, providing everyone with a nutritionally adequate diet is one thing; expanding the demand for farm food products is another.

Second, many if not most of the very poor are currently being reached with direct distribution programs through existing agencies. Third, the School Lunch Program now covers about one third of the school children, and those not covered are, for the most part, probably not seriously undernourished. And fourth, while the aged, on the average, may not have fancy diets, most are probably not seriously undernourished. They *are* eating, although our knowledge of their food habits is painfully lacking.

In sum, the expanded programs would (1) increase modestly the over-all food consumption of the average members of these vulnerable groups, (2) seek out and eradicate those relatively few cases of hunger or serious malnutrition where they now exist, and (3) make a modest contribution toward strengthening and maintaining the aggregate demand for food. But they would not give a big push to the aggregate demand for food.

The big and important market for food to be tapped in the United States comprises the 57 million persons falling within the income range $1000 to $4000 (since our categories are not mutually exclusive this grouping will include many of the aged and retired persons discussed above). There are a lot of consumers in this group and they are the consumers who rapidly increase their expenditures for food as their incomes rise. These are the people who with rising incomes shift cereals and pulses out of their diets and substitute more expensive animal products and fruits. The question is: *How is this broad market to be tapped?*

There is evidence to indicate that some farm groups have been successful in increasing the consumption of their particular products through advertising campaigns (particularly in the case of specialty

153

crops). But what may be a successful business policy for individual marketing firms and some farm groups is not necessarily a desirable economic policy for *all farmers*. And it will not be, to the extent that advertising is competitive — to the extent that firms and farm groups seek enlarged shares of a market of a given size.

What advertising can do is to sell more of that modern product, *food service*. The housewife is ever ready to buy more processing, packaging, and convenience when it enables her to escape from drudgery in the kitchen. Of course processors and food distributors like this, for it means selling more of the products that they supply. But selling more food services does not expand the demand for farm food products and thereby whittle down farm surpluses.

To expand the aggregate demand for farm food products through advertising and sales promotion, campaigns would need to convince the average consumer that he should, *within his present income*, substitute high-resource-using animal products for inexpensive food items and thereby increase his total food bill. To be successful, advertising would have to induce a fundamental change in the tastes and preferences of average consumers — persuade them to spend less for clothing, shelter, durables, hobbies, and recreation, and then to use the funds thus released to purchase more high-resource-using foods. In light of the higher income elasticities for the nonfood categories mentioned above than for food, *this change in consumer expenditure patterns seems highly improbable*. In short, average families will spend more for food as their incomes rise, but not more for food out of their existing incomes, unless that increase is subsidized.

Here is the nub of the market expansion problem. The potential market is there, but it is not a market to be captured in the near future without cost. The problem confronting society is the following one: Should society subsidize the upgrading of diets of below average income families? To date society has given its answer in the form of lack of interest in a policy that would cover the costs of programs designed to shift diets away from cereals, potatoes, and fats toward animal products and fresh fruits and vegetables. Society seems to attach great importance to a nutritionally adequate diet for everyone, but it does not value so highly a high-resource-using diet for everyone.

But the question may be asked: If society were interested, are there means for realizing the objective of upgrading diets? The answer is yes.

Several special currency or stamp plans have been developed to achieve this purpose, the best known being the Food Allotment Plan.[7] The cost of and the amount of participation in the Food Allotment Plan will depend upon two related factors: (1) how far up the income ladder the diets of family members and single individuals are to be upgraded, and (2) the cost of the diet plan defined as the food allotment. In a recent analysis of stamp plans by the United States Department of Agriculture [8] where (1) the income exclusion point for three member families is assumed to be $2000 and (2) the level of cost of the diet is assumed to be the Low-Cost-Adequate-Diet Food Plan of the Agricultural Research Service, it is estimated that some 15 million persons would be eligible to participate in the plan as of 1954. And if this maximum number of persons did participate, the total food costs of the plan with *constant prices* would amount to $1.5 billion. With prices constant total food expenditures would be increased $1.5 billion annually, or by $100 per participating family.

It has been further estimated that this increase in food expenditures by means of a stamp plan would induce an increase in total food expenditures at retail by $3.5 billion in the short run *because food prices would rise where supplies were fixed.* Total food expenditure at retail might be expected to rise from the original $1.5 to $3.5 billion through the competitive struggle of all consumers over a fixed food supply. And all of this $3.5 billion would be reflected back to farmers.

This $3.5 billion is, however, the maximum return that farmers might expect from an injection of $1.5 billion via a stamp plan. To the extent that supplies could, or would, increase in the short run in response to the stamp plan, the aggregate return to farmers would be less than $3.5 billion. But this is a good return on an original expenditure of $1.5 billion, so why not spend $1.5 billion year after year to increase returns to farmers by $3.5 billion year after year?

The trouble with this kind of program as an income generator for farmers is that it will *not* generate $3.5 billion for farmers year after year. Farmers will respond to the program by increasing total production with the consequence that farm prices will fall and in time materially reduce the farmers' gains from the program — possibly reduce them

[7] For a discussion of the mechanics and implications of the plan see the article by Rainer Schickele entitled "The National Food Allotment Program," *Journal of Farm Economics,* May 1946.

[8] *An Analysis of Food Stamp Plans,* Part B.

to zero. The major part of this reduction process might occur in two years, or possibly in five. The time period is subject to debate, but not the ultimate result. The short-run price-enhancing effects of the stamp plan would stimulate production and, through competition among the many farm producers involved, erode away the short-run gains from the program.

In the longer run, farmers would expand production in response to the stamp plan just as they have to the full employment economy of the past ten years. Neither is a guarantee of good prices and incomes to farmers. Once farm production was adjusted to full employment *plus* a stamp plan, a little additional output in the aggregate sense, resulting from the uncoordinated efforts of 3 million commercial farmers to increase output, would send farm prices and incomes tumbling down again. But just as we like full employment for its own sake, we might like a stamp plan that would upgrade the diets of below average income families for *its* own sake. Both are good in themselves, and both are helpful to agriculture in the sense of maintaining a strong demand for farm products. But neither separately nor together do they guarantee prosperity for agriculture.

In summary, nutritional adequacy for the poverty-stricken and other vulnerable groups may constitute a highly valued goal in the United States; but the increased food consumption approach to the price-income problems of commercial agriculture runs into several roadblocks. Advertising and sales promotion do not provide an easy avenue to increased per capita food consumption; for the industry in the aggregate sense this route is a mirage. Society has been unwilling to subsidize the upgrading of diets among the 57 million poor but not poverty-stricken consumers, which is where the remaining unexploited market for farm food products in the United States is to be found. Last, and most important, a large-scale program designed to upgrade the diets of low income consumers might shoot aggregate demand ahead of aggregate supply for a brief period, but the good prices that would result from this action would stimulate farm technological advance once again, and thus stimulate a burst in output expansion that would wipe out the early price gains. A one-shot stimulus to aggregate demand will not and cannot cope with the chronic American tendency to overproduce farm food products.

A Concluding Remark

The fact that the various policy approaches considered in this chapter are blind alleys — that they lead to more rather than less trouble — does not mean that they will not be traveled. One way to discover the existence of a blind policy alley is to pursue a course of action until it leads to a situation that is intolerable to society and its political representatives. This may be the way that farm people, and nonfarm people as well, will discover, *and rediscover*, certain of the blind policy alleys described above.

8

The Hard Policy Choices

Eᴀᴄʜ policy approach considered in the previous chapter ended in a blind alley for one reason — too much production. Too much production in each peacetime year since 1948, the capacity to produce too much currently, and the promise of too much in the foreseeable future have made a shambles of agricultural price and income policy in the United States. With the possible exception of the long-run wringer and all the suffering that it entails, no course of action has been devised which has the capacity to contain and then to direct the tremendous productive capacity of American agriculture along lines advantageous to both farmers and consumers.

In a letter to Senator Ellender which is almost defeatist in outlook Secretary of Agriculture Benson said: [1] "A technological explosion is occurring on American farms. Production per farm worker has doubled in the last 15 years. This creates a new dimension in farm policy and makes it virtually impossible to curtail agricultural output with the type of controls acceptable in our society." In short, farm technological advance has become a monster on the loose, which politicians and administrators despair of taming.

The key that can unlock the exits of the blind alleys of agricultural policy is perhaps to be found in one phrase of the above quotation from Secretary Benson: "a new dimension in farm policy." Perhaps a new way of looking at agriculture, involving a new conception of the place of agriculture in an industrial economy with new institutions of management and control, is called for. At least this is the thesis of this chapter; the technological explosion, the technological monster, in American

[1] Washington, May 2, 1957, U.S.D.A. 1377–57, p. 1.

agriculture *requires* a new dimension in agricultural policy. But if this is the case some hard choices confront society in general, and farm people in particular. It is the purpose of this final chapter to explore the nature and implications of these choices.

The First Choice

The first choice is not for farmers to make; it is a choice that all society must make. It grows out of the circumstances that since 1933 the money costs of supporting farm prices and incomes have been met by all of society, and that since 1951 the out-of-treasury costs of these supporting actions in agriculture have increased greatly. It is concerned with the question: Should all of society continue to underwrite the money costs of price and income support in agriculture, or should all of society bring this policy to an end? The issue may no longer be avoided; the magnitude of income transfers into agriculture from the federal treasury (i.e., from all of us) in the middle 1950s forces the choice.

The *net* treasury costs of the 1957 program of price and income support in agriculture (the program beginning July 1, 1957) are estimated in the President's budget request to Congress to be $3.8 billion: $2.5 billion for price-supporting and surplus-disposal operations, and $1.3 billion for the Soil Bank (*gross* treasury expenditures are estimated to be considerably larger, running up to $5 billion). The decision to transfer funds of this magnitude, and lesser but still large amounts in past years, into agriculture has been a tacit one — based on the hocus-pocus that those funds were not lost but were recoverable from the sale of government-owned stocks of agricultural commodities at some indefinable time and place. And two wars made this hocus-pocus come true.

But the decision by society to cover the treasury costs of price and income support in agriculture can no longer remain tacit. First, because wars have gotten out of hand, war is more likely to exterminate all life than to raise the level of farm prices. Second, because the rapid rate of aggregate output expansion, powered by farm technological advance, has made even moderate levels of price and income support in agriculture terribly expensive. An annual net expenditure of $3.8 billion, which is more likely to increase than to decrease in future years, has forced out into the open the debate, and the decision, as to whether society should continue to cover these costs of price and income support in agriculture.

Now it is possible that society, acting through its political representatives, will decide that it should continue to meet the costs of price and income support in agriculture. The rationale might run as follows: (1) we want a rapid rate of technological advance in agriculture to ensure abundant food supplies at relatively low prices; but (2) we recognize that the farmer, operating in the competitive market in which he finds himself, is in a weak bargaining position (i.e., is running on a treadmill); hence (3) in the interest of fairness and justice we should pursue a course of action designed to yield him a reasonably good and stable income. This is a possibility; it is what we are doing in 1957, and we may pursue this policy into the indefinite future. But the decision to pursue such a course can no longer be a tacit one hidden under the hocus-pocus of recoverable costs; the annual expenditures are too great.

If society chooses to defray indefinitely the costs of price and income support in agriculture, one approach — and a not unreasonable one — is the 1957 farm program. Stripped of its falderal, this program consists of three basic arms: (1) price support in the market place at roughly 80 per cent of parity, (2) production control and income distribution through the Soil Bank, and (3) disposal in foreign countries of stocks acquired by purchase and loan operations — foreign surplus disposal.

There are difficulties with this program. The Soil Bank, as a control device, has become a farce. According to Assistant Secretary of Agriculture McLain, farmers in 1957 will receive government checks for taking 26 million acres out of production, while actually reducing planting by only 12 million acres. McLain is reported to have said further:[2] "The department has the legal authority to close the loophole . . . if we felt that we could take the heat to do it." And it is well known that many acres were signed up under the Soil Bank program in 1956 that had already experienced crop failure. In other words, the Soil Bank in 1956 and 1957 has been used to distribute income rather than to reduce output.

The heavy emphasis on foreign surplus disposal raises problems too. The policy of giving food away, selling it for soft currencies, and selling it at a discount to foreign countries runs into opposition from at least two groups: competing export nations and the farm producers in the recipient countries. The first group fears, or sees, the loss of foreign markets resulting from the surplus disposal operations of the United States; the second group fears, or sees, a drop in their own farm prices

[2] *St. Paul Dispatch*, Monday, May 6, 1957.

as the result of the surplus disposal operations of the United States. Thus, pressure is generated in foreign countries to bring these disposal operations (dumping operations, as these two groups view them) to an early end. And where the United States has other foreign policy goals such as collective security this pressure can be highly effective. It is not easy to give food away, either at home or abroad.

These difficulties could be overcome at least in part. The Soil Bank could be administered with reasonable effectiveness if the administrators believed in its control aspects, and if farmers believed that reductions in output would be permitted to manifest themselves in price increases. But most important, the Soil Bank is not a policy for the faint-hearted. First, it is costly; and second, the will to reduce output must exist among both farmers and administrators.

The dumping aspects of disposing of surpluses abroad could be minimized if the federal government and the foreign countries involved entered into long-term agreements whereby the expanding farm output of the United States was geared to the development needs of the recipient countries. In other words, the foreign relations problems of surplus disposal could be minimized if the policy of disposing of *surpluses* were ended (i.e., disposing of wheat one year, dairy products the next, and cotton the next), and the food and fiber *needs* of underdeveloped countries were built into the aggregate demand for farm products on a continuing basis.[3] Further, some of the surplus could be shifted back to the United States. A large-scale food allotment program for the United States, designed to upgrade the diets of 20 to 30 million low-income consumers, would reduce the size of foreign disposal operations materially.

Assuming for the moment that society is willing to underwrite price and income support in agriculture in the amount of $3 to $5 billion per year, it would seem that the 1957 farm program could be made to "work" (i.e., to provide some income support to farmers, and not be overwhelmed by surplus stocks). Price support at the general level of 80 per

[3] For current thinking along these lines see the paper by J. T. Saunders of the U.S. Department of Agriculture entitled "Our Agricultural Surpluses — Problem or Opportunity," given before the Southwestern Social Science Assn., Annual Convention, College Station, Texas, April 1957; also *Uses of Agricultural Surpluses to Finance Economic Development in Underdeveloped Countries: A Pilot Study in India,* FAO of U.N. Commodity Policy Studies No. 6, June 1955; and the committee print entitled *Agricultural Surplus Disposal and Foreign Aid,* A Study Prepared at the Request of the Special Committee to Study the Foreign Aid Program, United States Senate, by the National Planning Assn., 85th Congress, 1st session, March 1957.

161

cent of parity would act as a modest drag on farm technological advance and provide a modest amount of price and income support. The Soil Bank program would act as a partial brake on aggregate output expansion, and put some extra cash in the hands of farmers. And the production overflow accumulating in government hands as a result of price-supporting operations would be distributed by means of continuing surplus disposal operations. The picture that emerges is neither a pretty one nor a tidy one. But conceivably it is a workable one.

If society chooses to cover the continuing costs of price and income support in agriculture, an entirely different approach merits consideration. This is the income payments, or compensatory payments, approach. Many agricultural economists and leaders have advocated this approach,[4] but George E. Brandow has perhaps presented the general idea in its most modern and appealing form. He outlines the main features of a modified income, or compensatory payments, program as follows:

The program described here calls for assigning marketing allotments on historical bases to producers. With certain exceptions, the total of producer allotments for each commodity is to be about 75 per cent of total marketings in a base period. Market prices are not to be supported nor production controlled. If market prices fall below intended prices, direct, compensatory payments are made on marketings not in excess of each producer's allotment. Quantities in excess of allotments may be marketed but return only the market price to the producer. The total marketing allotment for each commodity is fixed, but the total is distributed among producers according to sales over a three or four year period; consequently, allotments can shift slowly among producers.

Thus the attempt to use price for both income and resource allocation objectives is made by dividing each producer's output of each designated commodity into a major portion receiving income support and a residual portion on which the market value of marginal production is realized. The program is to include as many commodities as economic and administrative considerations permit. Twenty products are suggested for inclusion initially. The proposal is inherently an industry-wide program, and the allotments, unlike current marketing quotas, are not voted "in" or "out" by producers of individual commodities.[5]

[4] Perhaps the two men with whom the idea is most commonly linked are T. W. Schultz and Charles F. Brannan. For the Schultz version see *Agriculture in an Unstable Economy* (New York: McGraw-Hill, 1945), pp. 221–235; for the Brannan version see statement by Secretary Charles F. Brannan at a joint hearing of the House Committee on Agriculture and the Senate Committee on Agriculture and Forestry, April 7, 1949.

[5] "A Modified Compensatory Price Program for Agriculture," *Journal of Farm Economics*, November 1955, pp. 717–718.

Brandow recognizes that compensatory payments to farmers for the difference between intended (or fair) prices and market prices would induce an expansion in output. But he hopes that

Making compensatory payments only on allotment quantities will substantially reduce some of the difficulties [with regard to expanded output] while retaining the income support function. Farmers' decisions to expand or contract an enterprise will be governed mainly by the value of marginal output. "Errors" in establishing intended prices will be less damaging to resource allocation than in the usual case, and government expenditures on the program are less likely to get out of hand over a period of years.[6]

With regard to the level of intended (or fair) prices and cost and returns under the program as of 1954, Brandow has this to say:

Income considerations are of particular importance in establishing the *average level* of intended prices. The amount of money that Congress and the public are willing to see spent on farm income support imposes some upper limit on how ambitious the program can be, and indirect efforts on resource allocation will also be of some importance. It would seem reasonable to try to keep the purchasing power of net income of farm operators from falling much below the 1954 position. As data presented later suggest, setting intended prices at 90 per cent of modernized parity might have approximately this result.

Total income from marketings might be expected to decline from 30.0 billion dollars in 1954 to 26.4 billion dollars under the program. Direct payments [of $3 billion], however, would pull cash income up to within 0.5 billion dollars of the 1954 position; and reduced expenditures for feed because of lower prices might equal this amount. Income from meat animals and eggs would increase; income from food grains, cotton and tobacco would decline materially. The non-farm public would pay to farmers via the market and direct payments about the same amount as farmers received under price support in 1954, and in return consumers would obtain a larger volume and more desired combination of farm products.[7]

This is the rational approach to income protection for agriculture. The need for income protection in agriculture is openly recognized, income payments are distributed in an effective and equitable manner, and the advantageous aspects of a free market pricing system are retained.

In the setting of the 1950s *the approach does, however, have one important weakness.* Guaranteed prices at 90 per cent of parity for 75 per cent of each farmer's production would trigger a rapid expansion in

[6] *Ibid.*, pp. 720–721.   [7] *Ibid.*, pp. 721, 730.

aggregate farm output. At the reasonably good, *and guaranteed,* incomes that such prices would generate, farmers would have a strong incentive to adopt new technologies as they became available; they could finance them too, with the result that aggregate output would surge ahead of aggregate demand. As aggregate output outraced aggregate demand, the farm price level would fall and the money costs to the government of the compensatory payments would increase. A program involving payments to farmers of $3 billion, as of 1954, might well increase to $6 billion within a few years.

But all that has been said above with respect to the workability and limitations of the 1957 farm program and the Modified Compensatory Payments Program has assumed that all of society was willing to underwrite the continuing treasury costs of price and income support in agriculture. It has assumed that all of society, acting through the federal government, was willing to transfer into agriculture some amount, ranging from $3 to $6 billion, year after year into the indefinite future. This is a large assumption indeed.

In the judgment of this writer, it is something that society will not choose to do. The strength of Secretary Benson's policy position in recent years derives, in large measure, from the unhappiness, the tiredness, of society with the continuing and costly aspects of price and income programs for agriculture. Society wants to get out of the business of supporting farm prices and incomes; this is abundantly clear. And the overt decision to do just that may be nearer at hand than some people realize.

The Second Choice

If the nation is unwilling to underwrite the costs to the treasury of price and income support for commercial agriculture, then all the farmers who make up commercial agriculture are confronted with a decision of the most basic kind. The decision is concerned with this question: What course of action shall commercial agriculture pursue where it receives little, or no, income support from the rest of the economy? How is commercial agriculture to organize itself to live and prosper in an economic world in which it receives little or no income support from the rest of the economy? (Actually, of course, this decision will be made in the Congress where all society is represented, but it is assumed here that commercial farmers and their spokesmen will provide the leadership.)

164

Basically the alternatives are two. The first policy alternative is a return to the free market (or a drastic version of the flexible price support approach, which is really a free market with price steps by years). More precisely, this alternative means pursuing a policy in which each individual farmer is free to plant, produce, and sell what he wants, and in which each individual farmer accepts the prices and incomes generated in such a market. The second alternative is to control market supplies. More precisely, this alternative means pursuing a policy in which entry into agricultural production is restricted and supplies are adjusted *to* demand, commodity by commodity, year after year, to yield reasonably good and stable prices and incomes. These are the alternatives that agriculture must choose between: where agriculture "goes it alone" there are no others. This is the hard choice confronting commercial farmers.

After reaching the conclusion that nothing that the Democrats or the Republicans have developed in the way of a price and income policy for agriculture has worked, Secretary of Agriculture Benson in the previously mentioned letter to Senator Ellender issued agriculture an invitation to return to the free market (or a flexible price support program where prices would flex downward until they cleared the market, which again is no different from a free market except that the price slide has steps in it). Secretary Benson argues as follows:

We are in the midst of great scientific changes. Agriculture is able to produce abundantly, and appears amply capable of meeting our needs for food, feed and fiber as far into the future as we can see with confidence. No production controls acceptable to American farmers appear capable of choking off this abundant flow.

Since we apparently cannot legislate scarcity, we must learn how to live with abundance.

If any product is abundant, it cannot long be priced as if it were scarce.

If farm products are abundant, the need and the challenge is to build markets so that this abundance can be used. We cannot build markets by pricing ourselves out of them.[8]

Secretary Benson obviously finds the restrictions to individual decision-making that *must* be a part of effective production and market controls more distasteful than the low farm incomes that a free market would generate. Or, stated positively, he values, he prizes, freedom of individual decision-making in farming above good and stable incomes

[8] *Op. cit.*, Washington, May 2, 1957, U.S.D.A. 1377–57, pp. 6 and 7.

from farming. And in appraising the value systems of farmers he apparently finds that farmers generally share his system of values. Perhaps Mr. Benson is right in this; perhaps farmers generally do value independent decision-making about their farm operations above good and stable incomes from those operations. If this is the case, farmers generally *must* be prepared to follow the Benson logic and accept a free market policy. Farmers cannot have the best of two different economic worlds, unless the rest of society is willing to pay for this luxury.

But this writer is inclined to doubt that farmers generally value independence of decision-making in their farm operations more than they value good and stable incomes from those operations. This writer is inclined to believe that farmers generally would be willing to restrict the management decision area to realize higher and more stable incomes for that management function.

Sugar producers in the United States, for example, operate within the framework of a controlled industry, and they don't seem to be terribly unhappy or restive under the "burden" of those controls. In fact, sugar producers give every evidence of liking their program of supply control. Similarly, fluid milk producers, who have lived through the chaos of free market pricing for their product, seem to like the partially controlled markets in which they typically operate (i.e., the federal and state order markets). And although all is not perfection in the tobacco industry, tobacco farmers have given no indication in recent years that they would like to give up their rather rigid quota system. In sum, whenever and wherever farmers have become convinced that reasonably good and stable incomes were absolutely dependent upon production controls, they have come to approve and accept those controls.

The policy problem in agriculture in the 1950s is that most farmers, and urban people as well, don't know what to believe, or whom to believe, with respect to the economic position of agriculture. They are thoroughly confused about the facts and the relations of the agricultural situation, and are even more confused about the price-income-quantity consequences of alternative courses of action.

Farmers have lived so long under the myth of a self-adjusting or easily adjusted agriculture (whereas in fact agriculture is always out of adjustment) that they are unable to rationalize theory and fact, myth and reality. Political leaders of both parties, most farm leaders, and most white-collar farm experts have told farmers so many times that agriculture is basically "sound," but only a little out of adjustment (a maladjustment that a little tinkering with the price mechanism, or the imposition of some temporary controls, would correct) that farmers do not know what kind of fix they are really in. Farmers generally don't know that they are running on the agricultural treadmill, hence they don't appreciate the desperate nature of their situation.

Certainly few economists have tried to explain to farmers the reasons for the "feast and famine" aspects of their industry, and only very recently have farm leaders come to appreciate the output-expanding force of farm technological advance. In consequence, farmers have not been convinced that adjusting supplies *to* demand, commodity by commodity, year after year, is essential to good, stable prices and incomes. Farmers generally have followed the lead of their spokesmen and tolerated "temporary controls," while such cures as advertising, increased efficiency in marketing, and a modest flexing of price supports were going to restore the health of a basically sound agriculture.

But this much is clear: if farmers choose the supply control route, they must do more than tolerate production and marketing controls. They must come to accept production and marketing controls in the same way that they do driving on the right hand side of the road, paying their taxes, and sending their children to school. For the supply control approach cannot succeed unless the overwhelming majority of commercial farmers approve and accept it.

It is distinctly possible that farmers would come to accept production and market controls, comparable, say, to those in the sugar industry if (1) they recognized clearly the price-income implications of a free market course of action and hence were convinced that good and stable prices and incomes were dependent upon conscious and continuous collective action designed to adjust supplies to demand, and (2) farm leaders would exercise their leadership to show farm people different ways that supplies might be adjusted to demand, and the implications to farmers of following those different ways. In other words, it is contended here that once the fog of the "automatic-adjustment" myth is lifted, and farmers are able to realistically appraise the price-income-quantity consequences of this increasingly productive machine of which they are a part, they may want to place some effective production and marketing controls over that machine. They may want to control it by regulating themselves, and thereby convert low incomes into high ones.

Some Ideas on Production and Marketing Controls

Although most farmers in the United States have viewed in the past, and continue to view, production and marketing controls as a nuisance, three producer groups have come to accept controls over supply as a regular and continuing way of doing business. They are, as mentioned earlier, fluid milk producers, tobacco producers, and sugar producers. The supply control programs of fluid milk producers and tobacco producers will not be discussed here, because in the typical case each lacks the first and basic requirement of a successful control program, *namely, the annual determination of the quantity of a commodity that a given market will take at a price defined as fair to producers and consumers alike.*[9] This determination of the quantity that the market will take at some defined fair price is the indispensable first step in a control program, a step which if not taken usually leads to failure, and a step which by accident, or design, the sugar program contains.

In 1933 sugar was in trouble along with most other farm commodities. And it also had troubles peculiar to itself. It was then, and probably is today, a commodity that could not be produced in the United States without some protection.[10] In those far-off days of the 1930s, pressure developed to remove the tariff protection on sugar as a means of expanding world trade and expediting economic recovery. But mounting world sugar supplies in the 1930s would have engulfed domestic producers if all their protection had been removed. To prevent this, a special program was developed under the Jones-Costigan Act to reserve a part of the domestic market for domestic producers, and to share the rest of the market with foreign producers duty-free. The principal instruments for dealing with the sugar problem under this act were:

(1) the determination each year of the quantity of sugar needed to supply the nation's requirements at prices reasonable to consumers and

[9] Economists like to joke about a fair price, because they, in their finite wisdom, cannot define a fair price. But the idea of a fair price, or a fair return, is terribly important and terribly real in the body politic, where the power of government is invoked to assure fair prices and fair returns. The determination of a fair price is generally reserved to the legislative branch of government, and is arrived at through compromise and conciliation among legislators. For a discussion of this concept see Willard W. Cochrane, "An Appraisal of Recent Changes in Agricultural Programs in the United States," *Journal of Farm Economics*, May 1957, pp. 288–292.

[10] The question as to whether sugar should be raised in the United States, and how much, is not germane to this discussion. Assuming that the collective decision has been made to produce sugar in the United States, and in a specific amount, we are discussing the control program under which it is produced.

fair to producers; (2) the division of the United States sugar market among the domestic and foreign supplying areas by the use of quotas; (3) the allotment of these quotas among the various processors in each area; (4) the adjustment of production in each area to the established quotas; (5) the levying of a tax on the processing of sugarcane and sugar beets, the proceeds of which to be used to make payments to producers to compensate them for adjusting their production to marketing quotas and to augment their income; and (6) the equitable division of sugar returns among beet and cane processors, growers, and farm workers.[11]

In 1936 the Supreme Court ruled that the tax on processors of agricultural commodities was unconstitutional when used as a device to control production. Thus, provision 5 above was supplemented by an authorization to the Secretary of Agriculture to make payments out of the federal treasury from funds appropriated for that purpose. Aside from that change, however, and the to-be-expected continuous quota revisions, the sugar control program of the 1950s is still the program of the 1930s.

A brief review of the sugar control program of 1957 may perhaps prove helpful in thinking about the kinds of controls that might be applied to agriculture more generally. In the first place, the Congress has stated clearly the objectives of the nation's sugar policy. They are

1. To assure American consumers an adequate supply of sugar at reasonable prices.
2. To maintain and protect the welfare of the domestic sugar industry.
3. To promote the export trade of the United States.

The sugar program provides various tools for achieving these purposes. The basic tool is the annual determination by the Secretary of Agriculture of the nation's sugar needs. In making this determination, the Secretary's objective is to make available on the American sugar market sufficient sugar to meet the nation's needs at prices that are reasonable to consumers and that will provide a fair return to producers. This estimate of the nation's sugar needs varies from year to year, and frequently is changed during a single calendar year.

From this determination of the sugar requirements of the nation stems a system of marketing quotas. The total of all quotas equals the estimated consumption figure established by the Secretary. The law sets the pattern of these quotas for the various sugar-producing areas by speci-

[11] *The United States Sugar Program*, Agri. Info. Bul. No. 111, U.S.D.A., July 1953, p. 8.

fying the formula the Secretary must use in calculating the quota for foreign countries and domestic areas. As changes in the consumption estimate occur, the quotas change in accordance with the method prescribed in the law.

The size and distribution of these quotas in 1957 are as follows:

	Quota
Domestic Areas	*(in tons)*
Domestic beat sugar area	1,953,952
Mainland cane sugar area	601,250
Hawaii	1,090,496
Puerto Rico	1,140,253
Virgin Islands	15,549
Total domestic	4,801,500
Foreign Countries	
Cuba	3,001,295
Philippines	980,000
All others	217,205
Total foreign	4,198,500
Total domestic and foreign . .	9,000,000

Any system of marketing quotas requires some machinery to make sure that the various producing areas stay within their respective quotas. Since all imports must go through customs, it is comparatively simple to see that no foreign country exceeds its quota. Checks on domestic-producers for compliance are, however, more complex. The law sets forth five domestic sugar-producing areas: (1) the sugar beet producing states, called the domestic beet sugar area; (2) the mainland cane sugar area, which presently consists of Louisiana and Florida; (3) Hawaii; (4) Puerto Rico, and (5) the Virgin Islands.

Each of these areas must stay within its quota. Further, when it appears evident that supplies in one of these areas are likely to exceed that area's quota by a substantial amount, the quota of that area is allotted among the sugar companies of the area. For example, each of the beet sugar processing companies in the United States receives a marketing allotment which it cannot exceed. Each company must periodically report the volume of its sales to the Department of Agriculture, and severe penalties are imposed for selling more sugar during a year than the company's marketing allotment for that year.

In order to keep actual production as close as possible to the domestic marketing quotas, acreage controls are also imposed on farmers who produce sugar crops. Compliance with acreage controls is maintained by a system of conditional payments. A farmer who exceeds his alloted acreage forfeits his conditional payment. These payments are also used as an incentive for complying with other restrictive provisions of the sugar act, such as requiring the payment of minimum wages to field workers, providing certain specified working conditions, and abiding by a prohibition against employment of child labor.

It may be argued that domestic sugar producers accept these industry-wide controls because they know that they would perish without them. And this is probably true. The interesting point to be made here is, however, not that a producer group accepts controls rather than extinction, but that the position of farmers generally is similar to that of sugar producers.

Sugar producers and farmers generally are in the same fix — available and potential supplies would collapse prices and incomes in a free market situation. In a free market many producers in both groups would perish. But there is one difference: sugar producers know this; most other farmers don't. The price-income structure of the farm sector of the economy has been supported so long by the nonfarm sector that in the 1950s and 1960s farmers and their spokesmen have little comprehension of the income consequences of a free market for agricultural commodities. Some firsthand experience with a free market might convince a majority of farmers in a hurry that effective production and marketing controls were not such bad things.

Since sugar is atypical in American agriculture in that about half of it is imported, and further since the complex system of quotas used in the sugar program might prove unmanageable when applied to all of agriculture (i.e., it would prove difficult to integrate these commodity quota systems where every important commodity was controlled), let us look at a supply control approach that may be better adapted to the American scene in that it provides more flexibility at the farm level. Basic to this approach is the idea that agriculture be viewed as a public utility — a giant public utility composed of many, many small producing units acting in concert with the aid and consent of government to produce the quantities of food and fiber required by consumers, at a fair return to the producers involved.

In this view, government establishes the institutional machinery for, and grants the power to, agriculture to enable the many producers involved to produce and sell those quantities of farm products demanded by consumers at a fair price. For this grant of market power, government reserves to itself, as in the case of any enfranchised public utility (railroads, telephone companies, and gas and electric companies), the right to determine and fix rates and prices and thereby the right to determine fair returns to the producers involved.

Where competition has led to ruinously low prices and returns, poor service, or injury to certain persons or groups, government has historically intervened to regularize that competition, to equalize the bargaining power among contending parties, and to redress inequities. (Government was acting in this role when it brought the railroads under the control of the Interstate Commerce Commission, when it gave unions the right to bargain collectively, and when it has tried to provide commercial agriculture with price and income support.) Where the continuous and uninterrupted provision of a product or service was deemed essential to the well-being of the community, government has traditionally granted certain firms the monopoly right to supply the needs of consumers with that product or service, under the supervision of government with respect to such things as rates, safety, and quality: *it has created public utilities.* Now it is proposed here that the government adopt this general policy with respect to agriculture; first of all to ensure producers of reasonably good and stable prices and incomes, and perhaps in some later period, when circumstances require it, to ensure consumers of an adequate food supply at reasonable prices.

The main outlines of this public-utility approach to the price-income problems of agriculture were sketched by the author at a joint meeting of the American Farm Economic Association and the American Economic Association in December 1956.

1. It would be the responsibility of Congress to determine and set forth fair, or parity, prices for agriculture, as it does now. But in this scheme of things the role of parity prices has changed. No longer would parity prices serve as pegs on which to support farm market prices; rather they would serve as guides in the setting of national sales quotas. Thus, in the determination of parity prices for agriculture, the Congress would in fact be determining fair prices for both consumers and producers, and the needs and interests of both groups would have to be considered.

2. The United States Department of Agriculture would set national

sales quotas for each principal agricultural commodity in amounts which the U.S.D.A. had estimated would clear the market at the predetermined fair, or parity, prices. In practice this might mean the establishment of national quotas on each principal farm commodity moving into the marketing channel destined for human consumption (say 15 to 25 commodities). And these national sales quotas would, of course, vary from year to year as demand conditions changed, or as Congress redefined parity prices. To avoid, or to minimize, the difficult problem of integrating production controls vertically, national sales quotas would not be established for commodities typically consumed on farms, sold among farms, or sold to farms (e.g., feed grains, feeder cattle, baby chicks).

3. Each *farmer* at the inception of the program would receive a market share, *his pro rata share*, of the national sales quota for each commodity, based probably on his historical record of production. The farmer's share might be received in small denominational units, to which, for purposes of exposition, the name marketing certificates is given. And once the program was in operation it would be illegal for a farmer to market any commodity having a national quota except insofar as he had marketing certificates to cover the quantities involved. The number of marketing certificates would not be increased, or decreased, from year to year with changes in the national sales quota for a particular commodity. Rather each farmer could market an announced percentage of the face value of each of his certificates — a percentage in accordance with the national sales quota for the year. By this device the awkward problem of issuing and confiscating marketing certificates would be avoided for the bulk of agricultural production.

4. *Each marketing certificate would be negotiable.* Each farmer would be free to buy or sell marketing certificates as he saw fit. By this device freedom of entry and exit would be maintained within a controlled agriculture; and the individual farm operator would be free to expand production, or contract it, in light of local conditions, as *total output* was adjusted to demand at a defined fair price. The value of operating in a stabilized agriculture where product prices and returns were relatively certain and relatively good, and where long-range production plans could be formulated with reasonable assurance of materializing would, of course, be capitalized into these marketing certificates. The price of these certificates would become the cost of doing business in a stabilized agriculture.[12]

Many side programs could, and possibly should, be linked to this skeleton proposal. To illustrate, the United States might for a variety

[12] Cochrane, "An Appraisal of Recent Changes in Agricultural Problems in the United States," *Journal of Farm Economics*, May 1957, pp. 297–298.

of reasons — human welfare or international collective security — wish to subsidize exports of food to needy nations to help them in their long-term programs of economic development. Under such circumstances the national sales quota for any one year would be equal to domestic demand plus commercial exports *plus subsidized exports.* If the nation decided to establish and maintain a strategic food reserve, the requirements of such a reserve would have to be taken into account each year in the determination of national sales quotas.

In another direction, it might prove beneficial to both producers and consumers for the United States Department of Agriculture to operate a purchase, storage, and disposal program in connection with the general control program, under which in years of *below-average* yields government-held stocks would be put on the market to hold prices at the defined parity prices, and in years of *above-average* yields marketing quotas would be increased by a few percentage points and the excess supply would be purchased and placed in storage. This kind of bona fide storage program would serve to stabilize marketable supplies, and ease farmers' production problems arising out of weather uncertainty.

The supply control ideas under consideration here may be illustrated — be given operational content — for wheat. The multiple uses of wheat — food, feed, and export — make it a troublesome commodity. If a satisfactory plan of operation can be sketched for wheat, then it should be possible to formulate satisfactory plans for other commodities.

Let us be clear first that we are talking about a *national* plan for wheat; the power to control and hence restrict supply at the local or regional level for a relatively homogeneous product like wheat would be less than worthless. As indicated in the general proposal, a national sales quota would be established for all wheat moving into human consumption to yield a fair, or parity, price for that wheat in the domestic market. The parity price under consideration here refers to the average level of prices for all food wheat; clearly it would not be feasible to establish a fair, or parity, price on each type and grade of wheat. The national sales quota would include estimates for (1) domestic uses of wheat *for food* and (2) exports (commercial plus subsidized exports under various governmental programs).

Purchasers of wheat destined for a food use would acquire from farmer-sellers a coupon of some kind covering the quantities of wheat that the farmer-seller had a legal right to sell (the coupon would be a sort of bill of lading based upon marketing certificates held by the farmer). And, to make a long story short, flour millers would periodically be required to turn in to the government coupons covering all wheat they had milled into flour. Failure to account with coupons for all wheat milled would carry stiff penalties.

Under this plan of operation, wheat for feed would be sold by farmers in the free market for whatever it would bring (wheat sold for feed would not move under a quota, but would be free of quotas as in the case of all other feed grains). Thus, each farmer-producer would establish his *own blend price* for wheat by raising wheat outside his share of the national sales quota, and selling it for feed for whatever it would bring. The more the farmer produced in addition to his quota share the lower would be his blend price.

This seems like a reasonable solution. The principal market for wheat, human consumption, is stabilized, but the farmer who wishes to produce wheat for feed at his own price risk is free to do so. Of course, the necessary import restrictions to protect the fair, or parity, price on supplies moving into domestic food uses are assumed here.

A second plan of operation for wheat might consist of establishing a fair or parity price *first* for wheat as a feed and *second* for wheat as a food, and establishing also the corresponding national sales quotas for each use. The fair or parity price for wheat as a feed would probably be set somewhat above the expected free price for corn if other feed grains remained uncontrolled, or somewhat above the fair, or parity, price for corn if other feed grains were forced under control (this latter development should be avoided if possible, for it would introduce rigidities into the production of animal products that would lead to continuous and troublesome problems).

Under this second plan the farmer could sell only those quantities of wheat for feed covered by marketing certificates, as in the case of wheat destined for human consumption. In other words, the farmer would have two market shares and two sets of marketing certificates for wheat; one for wheat as animal feed, and one for wheat as food for humans. After the point of first sale, coupons would follow and account for only that wheat moving into human consumption. The incentive to acquire cheap feed wheat would exist for flour millers: hence the higher priced wheat moving into human consumption would have to be couponed at all stages, and flour millers and other processors of wheat for

175

human consumption could legally purchase only that wheat (or an equivalent amount) covered by coupons. The coupons, in other words, would differentiate and limit the supply of wheat moving into human consumption.

Either of these control plans should probably have a purchase and storage operation built in. A purchase and storage plan would give farmers confidence in the program in the beginning — give them some assurance that the fair, or parity, prices would be realized in the market. But it would be desirable for other reasons. First, experts in the United States Department of Agriculture, lacking omniscience, would misjudge demand conditions in the year ahead by varying degrees; therefore the government should be in a position to remove supplies from the market whenever national quotas turned out to be too large, and to pour supplies into the market whenever national quotas turned out to be too small. Second, farmers generally, owing to weather conditions beyond their control, might misjudge yields for the year ahead; yields might turn out to be larger or smaller than were expected. The government should be in the position to adjust upward the percentage allocation on each marketing certificate and to purchase the additional supplies involved, when average yields exceeded the expectations of experts in the United States Department of Agriculture; or the government should be in the position to put stocks on the market when average yields were so low that national sales quotas could not be filled out of current production.

In both of these control plans, exports of wheat are included under *one* national sales quota for wheat. In other words, a separate sales quota covering wheat for export is not established. It is not established because once a supply control approach such as is envisaged here is adopted to give farmers something better than world equilibrium prices for wheat moving into domestic consumption, most wheat exports would have to move under some kind of government subsidy. In this context wheat exports would be determined by international agreement, and only the federal government would have an idea of the amount of wheat that might move into export and at what price (this, of course, is really the case right now, and it is not likely to change). Hence, in setting the national sales quota for wheat as a food, the United States Department of Agriculture would estimate domestic food requirements at the determined fair or parity price and *add to that amount planned exports under various governmental arrangements.*

The question may be asked: Would this supply control approach provide wheat farmers and other farmers with good or satisfactory returns? Obviously an unqualified answer cannot be given. But we do know this: (1) Congress sympathizes with the plight of the farmer; (2) enlightened monopolistic action of this public-utility type is certainly in the American tradition; and (3) the demand for wheat and most farm products is highly inelastic. It therefore seems likely that the Congress, reflecting the views of society as a whole, would be willing to grant farmers the kind of market powers outlined here, and to permit them to use those powers to restrict supply. Such grants of market power would enable farmers to drive prices upward and to gain returns above those obtainable in a free market.

But it seems likely that Congress would be unwilling to grant farmers complete, unregulated monopoly powers; food is a necessity and the interests of consumers as well as of farmers must be protected. In the last analysis what we are talking about here is giving the many small producers in agriculture *the necessary bargaining power* to live in a world where bargaining power counts, but not giving them the power to starve the rest of us into submission.

Lastly the question may be asked: Under the supply control approach in any of its operational forms, aren't the costs of providing farm people with good, stable incomes simply transferred from the public treasury to the marketplace? The answer, of course, is yes. But the further question must then be asked: Aren't the good and stable incomes received by management, workers, and investors in the steel industry, the automobile industry, the chemical industry, the medical profession, and many, many others realized through marketplaces where supplies are consciously and continuously adjusted to demand to yield good and stable prices? And again the answer is, of course, yes. So there is really nothing strange about society's handling or covering the costs of good and stable incomes to various industries through markets where supply is controlled. It just seems strange to some people that farmers should want, and should realize, good and stable incomes through supply controlled markets. But should all of society decide that supporting farm incomes at good and stable levels out of the public treasury is to be preferred to supporting them through supply controlled markets, then there is the well conceived income, or compensatory, payments approach to fall back upon.

177

The Inescapable Choice

Intriguing as the mechanics of a program may be, it would be misleading to end this discussion with the mechanics of supply control. In the first place, farmers may not choose the supply control route. In the second place, if they do, controls may develop along different lines from those suggested here. And, in the third place, the particulars of production and marketing control must vary with the physical and institutional characteristics surrounding each commodity.

The key ideas of this volume are to be found in the general theory of the agricultural treadmill. The constituent parts of that theory — the high value that society places on technological development and adoption, the incentive to farmers to adopt new technologies and reduce costs in a competitive market, and the inelasticity of the aggregate demand for food — related in a causal sequence — explain the downward pressure on farm prices and incomes in the 1950s and in the foreseeable future. The propensity for aggregate supply to outrace aggregate demand, and the dire price and income consequences of that persistent peacetime development, find an explanation in the general theory of the agricultural treadmill.

Given the general situation in agriculture described by the theory of the treadmill, and the decision by all of society to discontinue or reduce materially the treasury costs of price and income support in agriculture, commercial farmers are confronted with an inescapable choice: they can either choke off the rate of aggregate output expansion through widespread losses and business failure under the free market approach, or bridle the rate of aggregate output expansion by the widespread acceptance and use of production and marketing controls. These are the alternatives, unless all society is willing to continue to underwrite the treasury costs of price and income support in agriculture. This is the hard policy choice confronting American farmers.

APPENDIXES AND INDEX

Supply-Estimating Equations

THROUGHOUT Chapter 4 it was assumed that agricultural commodity prices and outputs are generated in cobweb structures. The cobweb structural conditions are not satisfied perfectly by each agricultural commodity, but the economic structure of most agricultural commodities is of a cobweb form. Now the cobweb structure is a special case of a recursive system — a system in which price gives rise to output, output to price, price to output, and so on through time in an irreversible process.

We are concerned here with estimating one relation, the schedule of intentions to produce, in such recursive systems. And, as Herman Wold has shown,[1] reliable (i.e., reasonably unbiased and efficient) estimates of demand or supply in a recursive system may be obtained through least-squares regression analysis, where the cause variables are treated as independent variables and the effect variable as the dependent variable. Such is our procedure here. We estimate the regression coefficients of the schedules of intentions to produce by least-squares regression techniques, being careful to treat cause variables as independent variables and the effect variable as a dependent variable in the analysis.

All estimates are for the United States, for the periods indicated. Where the regression analyses are in actual numbers, the price elasticity estimates are given for the point of means.

SCHEDULE OF INTENTIONS TO PRODUCE FOR POTATOES
(1921–41, 1950–56)

Estimating equation (actual numbers)	$X_1 = 378.791 + .6308X_2 - 1.8351X_3$	
Standard errors of b's.................	(.2402)	(.1499)
Level of significance of b's	2%	.1%
Means 283.1	110.5	90.1

$$R^2_{1.23} = .9175$$
Price elasticity $= .246$

Where
$X_1 =$ Acres planted in current year, as an indication of intentions to produce, 10,000 acres.
$X_2 =$ Potato prices deflated by index of prices received for all crops for years t-1 and t-2, weighted equally, cents per cwt.
$X_3 =$ Yield per acre in current year, cwt.

[1] *Demand Analysis* (New York: John Wiley & Sons, Inc., 1953), Chapter 2.

The X_2 variable, deflated potato prices, in this regression analysis is not completely consistent with the potato cobweb model of Chapter 4. The causative price in the cobweb model is the previous year's price, whereas the causative price in the regression analysis is an average of the previous two years' prices. The use of the previous two years' prices in the regression analysis increases the coefficient of multiple correlation considerably, suggesting that the true cobweb model is somewhat more complex than that portrayed in Figure 14 of Chapter 4. Implied in the schedule of intentions to produce estimated in the above regression analysis and used in the cobweb model is that farmers plan to produce on the basis of an average of the previous two years' potato prices.

SCHEDULE OF INTENTIONS TO PRODUCE FOR SPRING PIGS (1921–56)

Estimating equation (in first
differences of logarithms) . . . . $X_1 = -.0019 + .3086X_2 - .3497X_3$
Standard errors of b's . . . . $(.0754) \quad (.0618)$
Level of significance of b's . . . . $.1\% \quad .1\%$

$$R^2_{1.23} = .5491$$
Price elasticity $= .309$

Where
$X_1 =$ Number of sows farrowed December 1, year t-1 to June 1, year t, times the trend values of spring pigs saved per litter, as an indication of intentions to produce.
$X_2 =$ Hog prices, average for July through November of year t-1, cents per cwt.
$X_3 =$ Corn prices for September through November of year t-1, cents per cwt.

SCHEDULE OF INTENTIONS TO PRODUCE FOR MILK, BY QUARTERS (1947–56)

Estimating equation
(actual numbers) . . $X_1 = -56.6747 + .0301X_2 - .0220X_3 + .0152X_4 + .0033X_5$
Standard errors of b's $\quad (.0847) \quad (.0208) \quad (.0021) \quad (.0009)$
Level of significance
of b's . . . . $\quad\quad\quad ...^* \quad\quad ...^* \quad\quad .1\% \quad\quad .1\%$
Means . . . . 100 $\quad\quad 100 \quad\quad 337 \quad\quad 5433 \quad\quad 23787$

$$R^2_{1.2345} = .7324$$
Price elasticity $= .030$

Where
$X_1 =$ Milk production by calendar quarters, seasonally adjusted, percentage of 1947–56 average.
$X_2 =$ Average wholesale milk prices, quarters q and q-1, percentage of 1947–56 average (seasonally adjusted).
$X_3 =$ Dairy ration prices, average for quarters q and q-1, cents per cwt.
$X_4 =$ Production per cow in pounds, annual production in year t used for each quarter in t.
$X_5 =$ Number of cows kept for milk; number on January 1 used for first quarter, numbers for other quarters interpolated from preceding and succeeding January 1 figures.

Again in this regression analysis the X_2 variable, wholesale milk prices, is not completely consistent with the milk cobweb model of Chapter 4. The current quarter's prices are included in the regression analysis, because it was reasoned that current prices must influence current milk production.

* Not significant at the 10% level.

182

APPENDIX TABLE 1. PROCEDURE FOR CALCULATING THE AVERAGE REALIZED NET INCOME OF COMMERCIAL FARM OPERATORS FROM ALL SOURCES

Description	Year								
	1947	1948	1949	1950	1951	1952	1953	1954	1955
1. Average realized net income of *all* farm operators from farming, including government payment [a]	$2927	$2747	$2389	$2276	$2682	$2660	$2649	$2357	$2268
2. Incomes from line 1 expressed as index numbers (1949 = 100)	122.52	114.99	100.00	95.27	112.26	111.34	110.88	98.66	94.94
3. 1949 average realized net income of *commercial* farm operators from farming [b]	...	...	$3028	...	...	...	...	...	...
4. *Estimated* average realized net income of *commercial* farm operators from farming [c]	$3710	$3482	$3028	$2885	$3399	$3371	$3357	$2987	$2875
5. Estimates of off-farm income [d]	679	716	740	764	825	926	934	910	993
6. Total estimated average realized net income of *commercial* farm operators from all sources	$4389	$4198	$3768	$3649	$4224	$4297	$4291	$3897	$3868

[a] *The Farm Income Situation*, July 17, 1956, p. 26, column 7.

[b] *Agricultural Economics Research*, April 1956, p. 53, column 4.

[c] The amounts in line 4 were obtained by multiplying the 1949 average realized net income of *commercial* farm operators from farming by the index number in line 2 for the relevant year and dividing by 100. Thus, the estimates of average realized net income to *commercial* farm operators from farming vary about the base year (1949) by the same proportion as do average realized net incomes to *all* farm operators as given in line 1.

[d] The values in line 5 were obtained by the same general procedure described for line 4. The off-farm income to commercial farm operators (as reported in *Agricultural Economics Research*, April 1956, p. 53, column 7) was adjusted by the index of the average off-farm income to all farmers (1949 = 100). Data for this index were compiled from statistics reported in *The Farm Income Situation*, July 17, 1956, p. 20, column 6, and p. 26, column 1.

APPENDIX TABLE 2. DATA USED IN THE DEMAND ANALYSIS FOR THE PERIODS 1929–42, 1947–56

Year	Index of Per Capita Food Consumption (1)	Retail Food Price Index (Not Deflated) (2)	Index of Per Capita Disposable Income (Not Deflated) (3)	Time (4)	Adjusted Index of Per Capita Food Consumption* (5)
1929	91.1	65.6	55.1	1	97.5
1930	90.7	62.4	48.8	2	98.0
1931	90.0	51.4	41.6	3	98.4
1932	87.8	42.8	31.5	4	97.8
1933	88.0	41.6	29.4	5	98.2
1934	89.1	46.4	33.2	6	98.4
1935	87.3	49.7	37.1	7	95.7
1936	90.5	50.1	41.8	8	97.8
1937	90.4	52.1	44.5	9	97.0
1938	90.6	48.4	40.9	10	97.7
1939	93.8	47.1	43.5	11	100.2
1940	95.5	47.8	46.5	12	101.1
1941	97.5	52.2	56.3	13	101.1
1942	96.7	61.3	70.4	14	97.5
1947	102.0	95.9	94.7	19	97.3
1948	99.1	104.1	103.4	20	92.6
1949	98.9	100.0	101.9	21	92.5
1950	99.9	101.2	109.8	22	91.8
1951	98.1	112.6	118.3	23	88.3
1952	100.4	114.6	122.1	24	89.7
1953	101.5	112.8	126.7	25	89.7
1954	101.4	112.6	126.6	26	89.4
1955	102.8	110.9	132.2	27	89.6
1956	104.0	111.4	137.6	28	89.6

* The data in this column were estimated from the following regression equation for each year, with the influence of change in income from the mean and change in time from the mean removed.

Regression equation .... $X_1 = 88.448 - .131X_2 + .183X_3 + .212X_4$
Standard errors of b's .... $(.081) \quad (.082) \quad (.150)$

$$R^2_{1.234} = .904$$

Where
$X_1 =$ Index of per capita food consumption.
$X_2 =$ Index of retail food prices.
$X_3 =$ Index of per capita disposable income.
$X_4 =$ Time.

APPENDIX TABLE 3. INCENTIVE INCOME RATIO IN THE UNITED STATES FOR SELECTED YEARS, 1910-55

Year	Net Farm Income (millions)[a] (1)	Adjustment for Retail Valuation of Self Supplies (millions)[b] (2)	Aggregate Wages (millions)[c] (3)	Interest (millions)[d] (4)	Est. Total Net Rent (millions)[e] (5)	No. of Man Units[f] (6)	Farm Incentive Income — Aggregate: Cols. (1+2) −(3+4+5) (millions) (7)	Per Man-Yr.: Col. 7 ÷ Col. 6 (8)	Nonfarm Incentive Income Per Man-Yr.[g] (9)	Incentive Income Ratio Col. 8 ÷ Col. 9 (10)
1910	$ 5,436	$1,041	$ 755	$ 426	$1,659	9,343,000	$ 3,637	$ 389	$ 785	50%
1920	10,626	2,047	1,790	876	2,557	8,934,000	7,450	834	1,517	55
1940	6,340	997	1,029	525	1,904	9,083,000	3,879	427	1,476	29
1947	19,899	2,240	2,808	1,300	6,095	8,157,000	11,936	1,463	2,904	50
1950	17,883	1,608	2,750	1,680	4,831	7,066,000	10,230	1,448	3,312	44
1955	15,910	1,325	2,750	1,840	4,886	6,272,000	7,759	1,237	4,193	30

a The Farm Income Situation, FIS–159, July 17, 1956, p. 21, column 5.

b Ibid., p. 31, column 3 minus page 34, column 6.   c Ibid., p. 34, column 9.

d Interest charged on all non–real estate productive farm assets (livestock, crops excluding Commodity Credit Corporation stocks, machinery, motor vehicles used in production). Data were taken from Agricultural Statistics 1952, p. 625, columns 2, 4, 5; Agricultural Statistics 1954, p. 432, columns 2, 4, 5; Agricultural Statistics 1955, p. 434, rows 2–4; Balance Sheet of Agriculture 1947, p. 2; Balance Sheet of Agriculture 1950, p. 3; Balance Sheet of Agriculture 1955, p. 2. The interest rate is based on estimates made by D. Gale Johnson in "Allocation of Agricultural Income," Journal of Farm Economics, Volume XXX, No. 4, November 1948, p. 748, column 2, for years through 1947 and upon data from Agricultural Statistics 1955, p. 492, column 10 for 1950 and 1955.

e Obtained by dividing "Net Rental to All Landlords" (Agricultural Statistics 1943, p. 412, column 3; Agricultural Statistics 1955, p. 481, column 3) by "Proportion of All Land Rented" (Johnson, op. cit., p. 746; 1954 Census of Agriculture, Volume II, Chapter X, General Report, p. 965, columns 2, 7; the 1955 figures are estimated from 1954 figures).

f The number of farm operators and family workers was divided by the total number of people employed in agriculture; the same was done for hired labor (Agricultural Statistics 1952, p. 637, columns 1, 3, 5; Agricultural Statistics 1955, p. 438, columns 1, 3, 5). The number of people 14 years of age or over employed in agriculture (Statistical Abstract of the United States, 1955, p. 187, columns 4–6; Labor Force, Employment and Unemployment in U.S., 1940–1946, Dept. of Commerce, Series P–50, No. 2, pp. 25–26; Current Population Reports, Labor Force, Dept. of Commerce, series P–50, No. 31, p. 16) was then multiplied by the respective percentages described earlier in this footnote to calculate the number of persons 14 or over (a) in the family labor force and (b) in the farm hired labor force.

The total hired farm laborers were added to nonagricultural industry employees to give the "total nonagricultural man units."

Farm operator and family labor figures were adjusted to man units by multiplying the data by the average number of hours worked on the farm and dividing this figure by the average number of hours worked in nonagricultural industries (Current Population Reports, Labor Force, Dept. of Commerce, Series P–50, No. 63, p. 1, columns 2, 3).

g See Appendix Table 4 for the relevant data and computational steps involved in the nonfarm incentive income estimates.

APPENDIX TABLE 4. NONFARM INCENTIVE INCOME IN THE UNITED STATES FOR SELECTED YEARS, 1910–55

Year	Personal Income (millions)[a] (1)	National Nonfarm Profit-Yielding Assets (billions)[b] (2)	Interest rate [c] (3)	Interest: Col. 2 × Col. 3 (millions) (4)	Farm Income (millions)[d] (5)	Total Non-agricultural Incentive Income: Cols. 1 – (4 + 5) (millions) (6)	No. of Man Units [e] (7)	Nonfarm Incentive Income Per Man Year: Col. 6 ÷ Col. 7 (8)
1910	$ 33,252	$ 88.5	6%	$ 5,310	$ 4,681	$ 23,261	29,641,000	$ 785
1920	75,730	252.2	6	15,132	8,836	51,762	34,119,000	1,517
1940	78,680	278.9	5	13,945	5,311	59,424	40,270,000	1,476
1947	190,522	474.7	5	23,735	17,091	149,696	51,554,000	2,904
1950	227,050	653.1	5	32,655	15,133	179,262	54,132,000	3,312
1955	306,100	993.7	5	49,685	13,160	243,255	58,012,000	4,193

[a] Sources: *The Farm Income Situation*, FIS–159, July 17, 1956, p. 22, column 3 (national income figures used for 1910 and 1920); *National Income 1954 Edition. A Supplement to the Survey of Current Business*, pp. 164–165, Table 4, line 20; *Economic Indicators*, March 1957, U.S. Government Printing Office, p. 5, column 1.

[b] Based on January 1 estimates. Sources: R. W. Goldsmith, *A Study of Saving in the United States* (Princeton: Princeton University Press, 1955–56), Vol. III, pp. 14–15, Table W–1, columns 4, 5, 6, 10, 17, 21, 22, 23, 25; and *Statistical Abstract of the United States 1955*, p. 308, columns 4, 5, 6, 10, 11, 14, 21. The 1955 asset figure was extrapolated from 1949, 1950, and 1953 estimates.

[c] Data taken from Johnson, *Journal of Farm Economics*, Vol. XXX, No. 4, p. 748.

[d] Column 1 minus column 3 of Appendix Table 3.

[e] See footnote f, Appendix Table 3.

Index

Date Due

SE

SI